WE'VE MADE IT *easy*

2007/08

pay less tax

Paul Lewis

To my father

Contents

The publisher would like to say a particular thank you to Fran Gonsalves and also to John Andrews and team at the Low Incomes Tax Reform Group for their valuable help in reviewing this book.

Published in 2007 by Age Concern Books
1268 London Road, London, SW16 4ER, United Kingdom
ISBN: 978 0 86242 430 5

A catalogue record for this book is available from the British Library.

Copyright © Age Concern England 2007

Edited by Ro Lyon

Cover design by Vincent McEvoy

Designed and typeset by Design and Media Solutions, Maidstone

Printed and bound in Great Britain by Bell & Bain Ltd, Glasgow

Author

Paul Lewis is a freelance financial journalist who writes and broadcasts widely on personal finance issues. He presents *Money Box* on Radio 4 and writes regularly for *Saga Magazine*. His work also appears in the *Scotsman, Daily Telegraph* and *Reader's Digest*. His other books include *Money Magic* and *Live Long and Prosper*. His next book for Age Concern, *Beat the Banks*, will be available from February 2008.

Introduction

Who wrote it?

I have been writing and broadcasting about personal finance for more than 25 years, and I have one job – to help readers and listeners keep more of their own money. Over the years, I have saved thousands of people hundreds of thousands of pounds by clear honest advice about how personal finance – your money – works.

Why read it?

It will save you money. Every year people pay hundreds of millions of pounds too much tax. I love tax and the complexities of it all. I actually look forward to Budget Day. This book will help you pay less. Not by cheating or lying or hiding things. But just by making sure that you pay the right amount at the right time. If you have paid too much tax, it explains how to claim it back. After all, it's your money.

Who pays tax?

Most people. If you're under 65, you normally pay tax on any income over £100 a week. If you're 65 or more, anything over £145 a week is taxed. Even if your income is less than that, tax is automatically taken off some things. Your bank or building society deducts 20% off interest on your savings, and money you earn or get from a pension can have tax deducted before you see it. These automatic deductions are often wrong – that can mean you pay too much tax.

Isn't it all horribly complicated?

With a bit of time and occasionally a calculator, I honestly believe anyone can understand tax.

Look at it this way. There's a tenner lying on the floor. Do you go to the effort of bending down and picking it up? Or just say 'Can't be bothered' and leave it there. The effort it takes to read this book is like bending down to pick up a tenner.

Deep down, tax is simple. But politicians, lawyers and accountants spend their working lives making it more complicated. That's their job and it helps all of them take money off us; sometimes when they shouldn't. This book will help you get back money you should never have paid in the first place.

What does it cover?

This book is about five major taxes that drain our bank accounts and which we can reduce:

Income Tax – around half of people aged 60 or more pay Income Tax. It is due on your income from pensions (including the State Pension), earnings, interest on savings, some social security benefits, and rental income if you own a rented property. This book explains tax allowances and the rates of tax, and shows you how to work out how much tax you should pay – and how to claim it back if you have paid too much. It explains tax codes and tax for people who are self-employed (pages 74–84). It also, of course, explains self-assessment, which can apply to people who are self-employed, have untaxed income from savings, pay tax at the higher rate of 40%, or in some cases just have an income above £20,900. In rare cases, some people who just get the State Pension are sent a self-assessment form.

National Insurance contributions (pages 51–55) – these must be paid by men under 65 and women under 60 if they work and earn more than £100 a week, or if they are self-employed and earn more than £89 a week.

Capital Gains Tax (CGT – pages 85–91) – very few people pay CGT each year, but it can sneak up on you. It is a tax on the growth in value of something you own and is normally due when you get rid of it – either by selling it or giving it away. It can also apply if you get a sudden windfall from a mutual insurance business when it converts from a society to a company.

Inheritance Tax (IHT – pages 92–101) – is charged on the money and property you leave when you die. Few estates are liable to IHT but, like CGT, it can take people with fairly modest means by surprise, and rising house prices mean that more people fear being caught by it. This book explains how to reduce the risk of your relatives losing out when you die, and the new rules that will mean fewer married couples will pay it.

Stamp Duty Land Tax (SDLT – pages 102–103) – often just called stamp duty, SDLT is normally charged on any home that is bought for more than £125,000. There are a few ways to reduce it.

These five taxes are collected by Her Majesty's Revenue & Customs (HMRC), which I call just 'the Revenue' in this book. Pages 68–73 give information about contacting the Revenue and what to do when things go wrong – as they often do.

The book does not cover taxes on things we buy, such as Value Added Tax (VAT), the duties on alcohol, tobacco, and petrol, airport passenger duty charged on air tickets or insurance premium tax paid on some premiums for some kinds of insurance. Nor does it cover stamp duty on shares or the annual road tax we pay for every vehicle we own. There is not much you can do about those taxes – except give up the things that are taxed.

It's not about council tax (or rates in Northern Ireland). That is set and collected by your local council and there are ways you can reduce the amount you pay. To find out how, contact the Age Concern Information Line on 0800 00 99 66 (8am–7pm, 7 days a week).

Is it up to date?

No book on tax can guarantee that the rules haven't changed since it was written. But the information should be accurate for the tax year 6 April 2007 to 5 April 2008. A lot of changes were announced in the 2007 Budget but they will not start until April 2008. There will be a new edition of this book soon after they begin.

As this book was going to press the Chancellor announced changes to Inheritance Tax. We have included details of these changes as far as we understand them. But the final rules may differ in detail after they have been passed by Parliament.

If you are completing a tax return for 2006/07 – which will normally have arrived in April 2007 – you will need to know last tax year's rates and allowances too. They are at the end (pages 104–107).

If you live abroad – or pretend you do to avoid tax – this book is not for you. The information in this guide only applies to people who live in the UK and are what the Revenue calls 'domiciled' here. That means the UK is where your roots – and your heart – are.

Paul Lewis

"Intaxication: Euphoria at getting a refund from the Revenue; which lasts until you realise it was your money to start with." (With thanks to a reader of *The Washington Post*)

Income Tax

Your income is assessed for tax over the 'tax year' which runs from 6 April to the following 5 April. If you want to know why that year is used, it dates back to the reform of the calendar in 1752 when 11 days were taken out of September to get the calendar back in line with the seasons. Those 11 days pulled the start of the year from 25 March to 6 April – but only for tax. The calendar year was moved back to start on 1 January.

This book covers the rules that apply for the tax year 6 April 2007 to 5 April 2008. Big changes in the rules are planned to start in the following tax year which begins on 6 April 2008. Those changes are not described in detail in this book. A new edition will be published in May 2008.

The principle behind Income Tax is simple. You are allowed a certain amount of income each year without paying tax on it at all. The rest of your income is taxed; and the bigger your income, the higher the rate of tax you pay on it. The detailed way in which the system works is very complicated, though, and often leaves experts scratching their heads. This section explains the rules and shows you how to work out whether you should pay any tax at all, and if so how much. It also explains how to claim tax back if you have paid more than you should have done.

Which income is tax-free?

Some types of income have no tax due on them. However much of that sort of income you have you needn't worry about tax. The Revenue calls it 'non-taxable' income and it includes:

- **Social security benefits that depend on your income** – they are Council Tax Benefit, Housing Benefit, Pension Credit (over age 60), and Income Support (under age 60).

Money-saving tip: *More than two million people aged over 60 do not claim the help they could get with their Council Tax, their rent, or their income in general. More than £2 billion goes unclaimed each year. Ask for advice at your local Age Concern or Citizens Advice Bureau, call the Pension Credit line on 0800 99 1234 or look online at www.entitledto.com which will help you work out what you can claim.*

- **Child Tax Credit (for people with children) and Working Tax Credit (for people in low-paid work)** have special rules to help those aged over 50 who return to work. Tax credits are paid by the Revenue but have nothing to do with tax. They depend on your household income and are paid directly to the householder or the main carer of the child.

Money-saving tip: *Tax credits are hard to understand and work out. If you have low pay or a dependent child, you may be*

able to claim. Call the Tax Credits Helpline on 0845 300 3900 (0845 603 2000 in Northern Ireland) or look online at www.entitledto.com which will help you work out what you can claim.

- **Most benefits paid because of a disability or illness** – these include Attendance Allowance, Disability Living Allowance (care and mobility components), Industrial Injuries Schemes Benefits, War Disablement Pension, War Widow's Pension, Severe Disablement Allowance, Independent Living Fund payments and other disablement pensions from the police, fire brigade, and merchant navy. Incapacity Benefit is tax-free for the first six months you receive it. It is also tax-free if you claimed it before 13 April 1995 and have claimed it continuously since.

Money-saving tip: *Lots of people could claim disability benefits but do not do so. When you claim, be honest about what you can and cannot do. Many people downplay their problems and that can stop them getting the benefits they are entitled to. Your local Age Concern or Citizens Advice Bureau can help you claim.*

- **The £10 Christmas Bonus** which is paid with the State Pension.

- **The Winter Fuel Payment** for people aged 60 or more.

Money-saving tip: *You can get the £200 Winter Fuel Payment this winter if your date of birth is 23 September 1947 or earlier. If you reach that age this year, the Department for Work and Pensions may not know about you. Call 08459 15 15 15 to let them know – have your National Insurance number handy. Look online at www.thepensionservice.gov.uk/winterfuel to find out more.*

- **The £2,000 Bereavement Payment** which a husband or wife may get when their partner dies.

- **Child Benefit**.

- **Some investment income** – including the gains on National Savings certificates, interest on an Individual Savings Account (ISA) or, if you still have one, a PEP (see pages 32–33).

- **If you rent out a room in your home, up to £4,250 rent in the year** is normally tax-free. The person you rent to must share your home, perhaps sharing the kitchen or bathroom and some living space, and must not be a tenant. You need not declare the income if it is no more than £4,250 but you cannot claim any expenses in connection with the let. Look online at www.hmrc.gov.uk/individuals/tmarent-a-room-scheme.shtml for more information.

- **Prizes from gambling** – including winnings on Premium Bonds, football pools, racing, and the National Lottery. But if you make your living from gambling, the income can be taxable.

Money-saving tip: *Don't gamble. The odds are always in favour of the bookie or casino and new higher rates of tax from April 2007 on gambling companies mean there is even less money left for them to pay out in winnings.*

- **Gifts** – even gifts of money you receive regularly. But if you are given money in exchange for doing work or providing a service, then that is counted as earnings and is taxable. In rare circumstances, a gift of money may be liable to Inheritance Tax.

- **Maintenance payments** made to a divorced or separated spouse or civil partner, or to children.

- **Dividends paid on shares** are taxed in a strange way. Tax is already taken off the dividend before you get it and there is no tax to pay for people who pay basic-rate tax or below. Higher-rate taxpayers will have to pay some tax on them (see pages 31–32).

- **If you are made redundant, the first £30,000 of any redundancy payment is tax-free and the rest is taxable**. But if you are entitled to a leaving payment under your contract of employment, then the whole of it will be taxed before you receive it. The Revenue may challenge the exemption on redundancy money if it considers that your redundancy was not genuine: for example, if it was in fact early retirement.

Tax-saving tip: *If the Revenue questions the tax-free status of a redundancy payment, challenge it. Get advice, as the Revenue does make mistakes.*

- **A lump sum for an injury or disability that prevents you from continuing to work.**

- **A payment made when you leave a job where you mainly worked abroad.**

Which income is normally taxed?

All other income may be taxed if you have more than a certain amount of it. The Revenue calls it 'taxable income' and it includes:

- **Wages, salary, and any other bonuses or payments given to you for work you have done.**

- **The profit you make as a self-employed person.**

- **The State Pension.**

- **Any pension from your job, any personal pension or any other pension which you have paid into.**

- **Social security benefits that replace pay** – these include Bereavement Allowance, Carer's Allowance, Statutory Sick Pay, Maternity Pay and sickness and maternity benefits.

- **The interest on savings and investments** – including any investments held abroad, apart from the exceptions listed above in the non-taxable section.

- **The rent you receive from property you own** – except for the rent-a-room scheme (see page 4). If you do not come under the rent-a-room scheme, then you can deduct any expenses before the income is taxable.

Incapacity Benefit is a bit more complicated, as mentioned above. If you claimed it for the first time after 12 April 1995 and you have received it for at least 28 weeks, then it is taxable; otherwise it is not.

What are tax allowances?

Each year we are allowed to have a certain amount of taxable income before any tax is due. These amounts are also called 'personal allowances' and every individual – men and women, married or single, living with someone or alone, aged 2 or 92 – gets one. Although they are called 'tax allowances', they are not an amount of money you are given – they are the amount of taxable income you are allowed to have before you have to start paying tax on it.

In 2007/08 the personal allowances are:

Tax allowances 2007/08	
Age 0 to 64	£5,225
Age 65 to 74 on 5/4/2008	£7,550
Age 75 or more on 5/4/2008	£7,690
Blind person – add	£1,730

So if you are aged 65 and your total income from earnings, pensions and interest amounts to £7,550 or less, then you should not have to pay Income Tax. If it amounts to more than that, then Income Tax will be due on the excess.

Income above your personal allowance is taxed at one of five rates, depending on:

- how much there is; and

- where it comes from.

The Chancellor said in his 2007 Budget "I can now return Income Tax to just two rates". But that was for next year – and even then there will still be four rates!

Rates of Income Tax 2007/08	
Income on top of allowance	**Rate of tax**
Up to £2,230 – starting rate	10% on all kinds of income
£2,231 to £34,600 – basic rate	10% on dividends 20% on interest and income from other investments 22% on everything else, including earnings, pensions, and rental income
Above £34,600 – higher rate	40% on all income (except dividends which are taxed at 32.5%)

Everything in tax has little quirks. So let's look at the allowances in a bit more detail:

People aged 65 and over

You can claim the higher personal allowance for a whole tax year (6 April to 5 April) if you reach 65 or 75 at any time during the year.

So if you were born before 6 April 1943 you can claim the higher allowance in 2007/08. If it was before 6 April 1933 you can claim the higher allowance for people over 75.

Tax-saving tip: *The Revenue should know your date of birth, but it does not always get it right. So if you will be 65 or 75 between 6 April 2007 and 5 April 2008, check that you get the right tax allowance this tax year. Normally the Revenue will not give you the allowance in the year you become eligible. It will give it to you the following year and sort out the overpayment then. So make sure you ask for it this year – if you ask, you will get it.*

But, and it is a big but, one of the most annoying things about this higher allowance is that you lose it if your income is above a certain level:

- £ The personal allowance will be reduced if what is called your 'total gross income' is more than £20,900. We explain how to work that out later.

- £ For every £2 of extra income above £20,900 your allowance will be reduced by £1.

For example if you are 65 and your total income is £21,900 your allowance will be reduced by £1,000 ÷ 2 = £500 to £7,050.

£ The allowance is never reduced below the basic personal allowance of £5,225.

£ It will be reduced to £5,225 if your income is £25,550 or more (aged 65 to 74) or £25,830 or more (aged 75 or over).

If your personal allowance is reduced because your income is over £20,900, you can end up paying tax at a very high rate. Income between £20,900 and £25,550 (£25,830 over 75) is in fact taxed at 30% or 33%. It works like this:

£ Each extra £2 of income is taxed at 22% (or 20% if it is investment income) and it reduces your allowances by £1, bringing another £1 of income liable to tax.

£ The result is that each £2 increase in income results in tax on £3 of income. At 22% that is 66p.

£ So for each £2 of income, your tax rises by 66p or 33%. If it is investment income, the tax rate is 30%.

Tax-saving tip: *If you are married, consider moving assets between you to make sure that neither spouse has an income above £20,900. The £20,900 income limit applies separately to the income of each member of a couple (see the example of Sid and Lillian on pages 64–67).*

Total gross income

If you are a basic-rate taxpayer aged 65 or over and you want to see if you are entitled to the higher tax allowances for your age group (see page 7), you cannot just add up the income you receive. We referred earlier to your 'total gross income' – now we will explain what that means.

Any savings income which has had tax already deducted must have that tax added back. That process is called 'grossing up'. Every £80 of net interest you receive is treated by the tax office as £100 gross income because £20 tax has been taken off it. **So to 'gross up' your net savings income, divide by 4 and multiply by 5.**

> **Matthew** *is 65 and retired from work in March 2006. His income for the year from State and occupational pensions totals £7,074. As he is 65, his tax allowance is £7,550. He also gets interest from a bank account, which he expects to be £464 this year. So he thinks his total income is £7,538, which is just below his tax allowance, and he expects to pay no tax. But he has forgotten to gross up his additional income from interest. If he divides it by 4 and multiplies by 5, he gets £580, which takes his total income up to £7,654. Tax will be deducted from all his savings income. But he will be able to claim a repayment of some of it (see pages 30–31 for more details).*

If you get dividends on shares, then you must also use the gross dividend to work out if you are entitled to the higher allowance.

On the other hand you can deduct some income. You can take off any payments to charity made under Gift Aid. Because Gift Aid payments come out of your taxed income, you must work out the amount before tax and you do that by dividing by 0.78 (don't ask how to do that – get a calculator!).

£ So if you paid £100 under Gift Aid, you divide by 0.78 which gives £128.20 and you can deduct that from your income (there is more on Gift Aid on page 19).

You can also deduct any payments you make yourself into a pension scheme. Again, work out the amount before tax. Remember you can pay into a pension up to age 75 regardless of whether you are retired or not.

Only after grossing up your interest, and deducting gift aid and pension contributions, can you assess whether you are entitled to a higher allowance and how much it will be.

Blind Person's Allowance

A person registered as blind with their local authority gets an extra tax allowance of £1,730. That means a blind person can have an extra £1,730 income in 2007/08 before starting to pay tax.

£ So someone aged 74 who is blind can have an income of £7,550 + £1,730 = £9,250 before any tax is due.

A married blind person whose income is too low to use up the tax allowance can transfer it to their spouse or civil partner. If both partners are blind, they can each get the £1,730 and either one can transfer it to the other if they cannot use it in full.

Tax-saving tip: *If you or your spouse is blind, make sure you get the extra allowance.*

You may be able to register as blind with your local council even when you are not totally without sight. To be registered, you must show that your lack of sight makes it impossible to perform any work for which eyesight is essential. The Revenue can also give you the allowance if you have applied to be registered as blind but this has not yet been granted. You do not, though, get the Blind Person's Allowance if you are registered with your local council as partially sighted. The rules and procedures about registration are different in England, Wales, Scotland and Northern Ireland, so contact your local council for more details.

Married Couple's Allowance

The Married Couple's Allowance was abolished in April 2000 for most married couples. But some older couples can still get it if either partner was born before 6 April 1935 – so one partner has to be at least aged 72 throughout the tax year 2007/08. To qualify for the Married Couple's Allowance the couple must live together and, of course, be married or civil partners.

Since 5 December 2005, two men or two women can form a 'civil partnership' which essentially gives them all the rights and responsibilities of marriage. It is not called marriage and they are not called spouses (or husbands or wives come to that). Whenever this book refers to marriage or spouses, it includes civil partnerships and civil partners, most of whom think of themselves as married spouses anyway.

Despite its name, the Married Couple's Allowance is not like the personal allowance. It is simply a deduction off the tax that is due.

It is set at two levels, depending on the age of the older partner on 5 April 2008:

Married Couple's Allowance 2007/08		
Age of older partner on 5/4/08	Allowance	Tax deduction
72–74	£6,285	£628.50
75 or more	£6,365	£636.50
Minimum amount	£2,440	£244.00

The deduction is made after the tax due for the year is worked out.

The Married Couple's Allowance is available to those who marry or form a civil partnership now, as long as at least one of the partners was born before 6 April 1935. If the marriage takes place before 6 May, the full allowance is available in the year they marry. If they marry on or after 6 May, the allowance is reduced by one-twelfth for each whole 'tax month' starting on the 6th of each month. In subsequent years they get the full allowance.

Which partner gets the Married Couple's Allowance depends on when they were married:

- **For married couples who qualified before 5 December 2005**, the Married Couple's Allowance is given to the husband. But a married woman can choose to have up to £1,220 of it herself if she asks (worth £122 off her tax) and can have £2,440 (worth £244 off her tax) with her husband's consent (it may be the 21st Century but these are 20th Century rules!). The rest has to be taken off the husband's tax.

- **For couples (married or civil partners) who first qualified for the Married Couple's Allowance on 5 December 2005 or later**, it is given to the partner with the higher income. The other partner can choose to have up to £1,220 of it if they ask (worth £122 off their tax) and can have £2,440 (worth £244 off their tax) with the other partner's consent. The balance has to be taken off the entitled partner's tax.

Any change in the allocation of the Married Couple's Allowance under this rule must be done before the start of the tax year, so it is too late now for 2007/08 but you could do it for 2008/09. Once you have made the choice it will continue to operate until you make a different choice.

Get Revenue Form 18, Transferring the Married Couple's Tax Allowance.

Under a separate rule, a partner who gets the Married Couple's Allowance can transfer some or all of it to the other partner if their own income is too low to make use of it. That might be useful if a wife has a higher income than her husband does and he pays very little tax or none at all.

This transfer is made using form 575 Notice of transfer of surplus Income Tax allowances *(which you can get online at www.hmrc.gov.uk/forms/575-t-man.pdf). It can be done up to six years afterwards, so in 2007/08 you can look back to 2001/02 to adjust the allocation of the Married Couple's Allowance.*

Gerard *is 76 and his wife* **Clara** *is 71. Gerard has a State Pension of £95.60 a week and a pension from his job of £223.62 a month. They have no savings. His total annual income is £7,653.64. He is over 75 and his income is below his personal allowance of £7,690. So he has no tax to pay and cannot use the Married Couple's Allowance deduction.*

Clara has her own State Pension of £75 a week and a pension from her job in the civil service of £621.34 a month. So her annual income is £11,356.08. As she is 71, she gets a personal allowance of £7,550 and pays tax of £569.74 this year.

But if they ask to transfer the Married Couple's Allowance to Clara, she gets the full £636.50 deducted off her tax, so she pays none at all (saving her more than £47 a month). She asks for that to be done for earlier years too – right back to 2001/02 – and they get a cheque from the Revenue for more than £2,000.

The transfer is unlikely to be of use to people who first qualify from 5 December 2005, as the partner with the higher income will automatically be the one who is entitled to the Married Couple's Allowance.

But – just as with the higher personal allowances – the Married Couple's Allowance is reduced if the entitled partner's income exceeds a certain amount.

£ The calculation depends on how old each partner is, but normally it is reduced if the entitled partner's income exceeds £25,550 (aged 72 to 74) or £25,830 (aged 75 or more).

Once income is more than £33,240 (£33,680 if over 75), the Married Couple's Allowance is reduced to £2,440 and there it stays – it cannot be reduced further.

The allowance is only reduced as a result of the level of income of the entitled partner even if the other partner gets some of the allowance. The rules about working out your total gross income are the same as for the personal allowances and are explained on page 11.

Widows and widowers

There are no particular tax concessions for widows. A woman or a man who becomes widowed can continue to receive any Married Couple's Allowance that is due for that tax year, as can a bereaved civil partner. They can also receive any unused part of the Married Couple's Allowance that their partner was entitled to in that year. The deceased person's executors should make sure it is transferred.

Divorce

The Married Couple's Allowance is only available to married couples who live together. If a couple permanently separate, the allowance continues for the rest of that tax year and then stops. Normally the divorce will come after that and the allowance will already have stopped. But if a couple divorces without separating first, then the allowance stops in the tax year after the divorce.

If you make maintenance payments they come out of your taxed income. There are no tax concessions unless one of the former partners was born before 6 April 1935 and the payment is made under a court order, a legally binding agreement, or an order of the Child Support Agency. In these circumstances the person who makes the payment can get a deduction off their tax of 10% of the value of the payment, up to a maximum of £244.

If you receive a maintenance payment of any sort you do not have to pay tax on it.

Mortgage payments and home income plans

Interest payments on a mortgage do not qualify for tax relief.

But if you have a home income plan you took out before 9 March 1999, then the payment of interest on the first £30,000 of that mortgage is reduced by tax relief:

- 💷 For every £1 you pay the Revenue chips in 30p.

This amount is already taken into account as part of the payment you make and does not affect your other tax calculations.

Pension contributions

If you leave a job after less than six months, you will get a refund of the contributions you have paid into your employer's pension scheme. You can claim the refund if you have been paying into the scheme for less than two years – though that is probably not a good thing to do. Tax at 20% (or 40% on amounts over £10,800) will be deducted from the refund before it is paid to you.

Payments to charity

When you give any money to a charity, you will often be asked to make the donation under 'Gift Aid' rules. These rules enable the charity to claim back the basic-rate tax you have already paid on the gift.

> £ That boosts what you pay to the charity by more than 28% – if you give £10, the Chancellor will add £2.82 to your gift.

Gift Aid only works if you pay as much tax as the tax relief on your gift. If you do not pay tax, then you cannot pay through Gift Aid. If you do, the Revenue will try to recover the tax wrongly paid back to the charity, and the charity may try to recover from you the full amount you promised.

Tax-saving tip: *If you pay higher-rate tax, keep a receipt for any money you pay to a charity – including a single gift, however small, or a regular subscription. You can reclaim the higher-rate tax, which equals 23% of the amount you gave, through your self-assessment tax return.*

How is income taxed?

Income and tax is assessed over the whole tax year and in some ways it would be easier to pay none all year and then a lump sum at the end. But the Revenue likes to get its hands on our money as soon as it can – preferably without asking us first – and it has devised several ways of doing just that.

Earnings and pensions

The most thorough of these automatic tax systems is called 'PAYE' or Pay As You Earn – though it also applies to pensions. A recent study by the Revenue done for the National Audit Office estimated that each year the Revenue deducts £500 million more tax than it should through PAYE.

PAYE covers wages and salaries, as well as payments of pensions from a previous job or a personal pension or retirement annuity contract we have paid into.

If you are self-employed, your profits will be taxed through the self-assessment system, described on pages 42–51, but your pension or any earnings will normally still be taxed through PAYE.

PAYE uses a system called a 'tax code', which your employer or pension payer uses to work out how much tax to deduct from your weekly or monthly payment. Tax codes are explained in more detail on pages 34–42.

Under PAYE, your annual tax allowance is divided by 12 (or 52 if you are paid weekly) so that each month (or week) you get some income free of tax, and the rest is taxed.

£ So if your personal tax allowance was £5,225 and you had no other taxable income, your employer would not tax the first £435.41 you earned each month but then would tax the rest.

Tax-saving tip: *A tax code is simply an approximate way of collecting tax; it is not an accurate way of assessing what you should pay. So you may end up with too much tax deducted from your money. Always check the code when you receive it and check the amount of tax you have paid at the end of the year.*

When you leave work

When you retire from work, your income will usually fall. If that happens during the tax year, you may qualify for a tax rebate – that is because the tax code system assumes you are paid much the same all year. So if your income drops, you may have had too much tax deducted in the first part of the year.

If the State Pension is your only income when you retire, send your P45 form to your tax office, along with details of your age, the date you retired, and your estimated total income from the day you retire until the next 5 April. If any refund is due, it will normally come directly from the tax office.

If you get a pension from a former employer, any tax rebate to which you are entitled for the tax year in which you retired will normally be paid by reducing the tax due on your occupational pension. If your pension provider does not receive enough information to do this by the end of the tax year in which you retired, any rebate will normally come direct from the tax office. Don't expect it to come automatically – write to the tax office if you think a repayment is due.

Tax-saving tip: *If your income falls significantly during the tax year, make sure that the tax office knows as soon as possible.*

Retirement annuity contracts

If you started paying into a pension before 1 July 1988, it may be a retirement annuity contract (sometimes called a section 226 pension). They were personal pensions before that term was invented and you could have paid into one independently of your job or, if your employer did not have its own occupational pension, through your work. It may have been linked to a life insurance policy.

Until April 2007 these retirement annuity contract pensions (RACs) were taxed in a special way. Instead of using a tax code, basic rate tax of 22%

was deducted automatically from the whole payment regardless of other income or what rate of tax you paid. As a result many people ended up paying too much tax. They could claim it back each year, though many did not. If no tax was due on the RAC then a form called R89 could be signed so the pension was in future paid gross without tax being deducted. Again, many failed to fill in this form. Higher-rate taxpayers paid the extra tax due through their self-assessment form.

It was a rough and ready system and many of the 1.2 million people involved paid the wrong tax. So, from April 2007, RACs were brought into the PAYE system. In theory that is a good thing. It should have made sure that the tax deducted was more accurate for everyone. But the changeover was managed very badly – many people were given the wrong code, the tax deducted was wrong, and the helpline went into meltdown.

Tax-saving tip: *If you receive a pension that you started paying into before 1 July 1988, make sure that the tax now being deducted through PAYE is correct.*

People who had previously paid too much tax can reclaim the overpayment back to 2001/02 if they make the claim before 31 January 2008.

Tax-saving tip: *If you pay less tax under the new system, that probably means you may have paid too much in the past. Consider claiming a refund – and do it before 31 January 2008.*

The State Pension and benefits

The State Pension is taxable but is paid without tax being deducted. So it uses up some of your tax-free personal allowance. The Revenue deducts it from your allowance to get your tax code. That makes it seem that you are being taxed heavily on your earnings or private pension.

Even if you only have the State Pension you may have to pay tax, especially if you are a woman under 65 who gets a lower personal allowance. That is because the State Pension – including the earnings-related SERPS – may be enough by itself for tax to be due on it. If you have no other pension or earnings, then the tax will have to be paid through the self-assessment scheme (see pages 42–51).

The State Pension paid to a married woman aged 60 or more, whether based on her own contributions or her husband's, counts as her income. But if a married man gets extra State Pension for his wife who is under State Pension age, then that is taxed as part of his income.

Paul *is 65 and his wife* **Mary** *is 59 and does not work. Because Mary is under 60, Paul claims an extra £52.30 on his pension for her. It is called an Adult Dependency Increase. This extra pension is taxed as his income. But once Mary reaches 60, this extra pension stops. At that point Mary can claim a pension on her own contributions but she only has a very small amount due. So she claims a married woman's pension of £52.30 on Paul's National Insurance*

> *contributions. It is paid to her and is counted as her income when tax is worked out.*

Similar rules apply in the rare cases where a woman gets an Adult Dependency Increase for her husband.

Money-saving tip: *If you received Child Benefit for your children after April 1975, you may be entitled to Home Responsibilities Protection (HRP). That is a complicated way to give you a slightly higher pension for the time you spent caring for your children. Many women don't get the correct HRP allocated to them. Make sure the Department for Work and Pensions knows when you were getting Child Benefit and ask them to check that you are receiving the correct pension.*

Other taxable social security benefits (see page 6), such as Bereavement Allowance or Incapacity Benefit (in some circumstances), may be less than your tax allowances, in which case no tax is due. But if you are liable for Income Tax, it will be collected by adjusting your tax code if you have another source of income such as an occupational pension. In rare cases where one of these benefits is more than your tax allowance by itself, it can be paid with the Income Tax already taken off.

Money-saving tip: *If you are a married woman, you may have paid some full contributions before you were married. That can entitle you to a pension in your own right, which you can claim at 60. If you worked between 1961 and 1975, you will also have earned some graduated retirement benefit (Graduated Pension) and work from April 1978 can entitle you to an earnings-related pension if you were paying full National Insurance contributions. Contact the Pension Service to make sure officials know about all your previous jobs and addresses so they can give you the correct pension.*

The Age Concern book Your rights to money benefits *explains all about State pensions and benefits. If you want to contact the Pension Service, you can ring 0845 606 0265 and you will be connected to the pension centre covering your area, or look online at www.thepensionservice.gov.uk*

If you have a pension from abroad, it will be paid without tax being deducted in the UK. There is a special concession on most pensions paid from abroad which means that only 90% of the amount is taxable. If you get a pension from abroad, it is likely you will be sent a self-assessment form. Your tax office or a Revenue Local Enquiry Centre (see page 71) can tell you more about tax on pensions or other income from abroad. Alternatively, the tax on the pension may be collected by adjusting your tax code.

 Tax-saving tip: *If you get a pension from abroad, make sure that the 10% deduction is applied and check the amount of tax you pay at the end of the year – mistakes are common.*

Savings and investments

Interest paid on savings or investments is taxed in two different ways. Some interest is paid 'gross' – in other words, without tax being deducted first. If you pay tax, you will have to pay the tax on it later. But most interest and investment income is paid with the tax already deducted. Tax on dividends paid on shares is taxed in a peculiar way, explained on pages 31–32. Of course, some types of interest are tax-free – they are listed on pages 2–6.

Interest paid gross

Some sorts of interest are paid gross. Interest from most taxable National Savings & Investments products is paid gross. But interest on its Fixed Rate Savings Bonds is paid with tax already deducted. The interest paid on government stock, also called 'gilts', is paid gross unless you specifically ask for it to be paid net of tax. If you have money invested in a bank or building society outside the UK, then interest on that will normally be paid gross too.

Pain-saving tip: *Some people who were tempted by adverts to put money offshore to get the interest paid gross may think that means no tax was due. Sadly it does not. The Revenue now has new powers to track down offshore savings. So let the Revenue know if you have undeclared money abroad. It will be painful. But less painful than if the Revenue catches you first.*

If your total income is too low for you to pay tax, then you will not have to worry about paying tax on income paid gross. But if you have to pay tax, this will be done in one of two ways. If you pay tax on earnings or a pension through PAYE and the gross amount of interest you receive totals less than £2,500, the tax on it can be collected through your PAYE code. If not, you will be sent a self-assessment tax form to account for the tax due (see pages 42–51). If the tax is paid through your tax code the amount collected is likely to be approximate, so check at the end of the year that the right amount has been taken.

Tax on interest

The basic rate of tax for income from savings is 20%. This rate applies to almost all types of income from savings, including interest on bank and building society accounts, taxable National Savings products, and annuities that you purchase as an investment (called purchased life annuities – see page 33), but not retirement annuities that you have to buy with a pension fund, which are taxed at the same rate as earnings.

But if your total income is low – within a couple of thousand pounds of your personal allowance – you may only have to pay a lower, starting rate of tax, which is 10%. It applies to the first £2,230 of taxable income, including income from savings.

If your income is high – above £39,825 in the year – you will normally have to pay higher-rate tax, which is 40%, on your savings income. As 20% will already have been deducted, you will have another 20% of the gross amount to pay.

Joint savings of husbands and wives

If a married couple or civil partners have savings or investments in their joint names, any income will normally be split equally when the tax is worked out. But if they own the savings or investment in unequal shares they can make a joint declaration setting out how it is owned. Each will then be taxed on their actual share of the income. It is only worth making the declaration if that will reduce the tax you pay. That will happen if the person who actually owns most of the income pays a lower rate of tax than the other partner.

Tax-saving tip: *A couple may be able to save tax by transferring savings to the partner who pays no tax or tax at a lower rate. (See the example of Sid and Lillian on pages 64–67.) If you do not want to transfer the money but have a joint account with a partner whose total income is too low to pay any tax, you should only pay tax on half the interest.*

Bank and building society accounts

Interest paid on money you have in a bank or building society account has 20% tax deducted from it automatically. The basic rate of tax on savings income is 20%. Even if you are not liable to pay tax, or liable to pay it only at the lower 10% rate, the bank or building society will deduct tax at the full 20% without asking you. It's not their fault: it's the law!

If your income is too low for you to pay tax, then you can apply for the interest to be paid gross – without tax being deducted. So if you expect your total gross income for the year to be less than your tax allowances, apply to have the interest paid gross.

You do this by completing form R85, which is available from your bank or building society, a tax office or online at www.hmrc.gov.uk/forms/r85.pdf

You may need to fill in a separate form for each of your accounts. If you have a joint account, then any of the account holders who is a non-taxpayer can fill in the form. For example, if the husband pays tax and the wife does not, then half the interest can be paid tax-free.

Tax-saving tip: *Check your bank and building society accounts to see how much tax has been deducted. If too much has been taken off, you can get it back for up to six tax years using form R40 – you will need one form for each year for*

*which you are claiming tax back and one
each if you have joint savings. You can
download the form at
www.hmrc.gov.uk/forms/r40.pdf*

Even if you are liable to pay tax only at the 10%
rate on some or all of your savings interest, the full
20% rate will be deducted and you will have to
claim back the tax that has been overpaid.
Similarly, if you are a non-taxpayer but you have
not asked for the bank or building society to pay
the interest gross, then you will have to apply for a
refund of any tax overpaid. You can make an
application if you have overpaid tax in the last six
years, back to the year 2001/02 (although for that
year you have to apply by 31 January 2008).

Dividend income

If you own shares, you will normally be paid a
dividend once or twice a year. These dividends are
taxed in a peculiar way. You will be sent the
money net of basic-rate tax. But the basic rate on
dividends is only 10%. So if your dividend is £100,
you will be sent £90 (£100 minus £10), and the
document that accompanies the cheque will also
show what is called a 'tax credit' of £10, showing
you have paid £10 tax. If your income is not high
enough to pay tax, you cannot claim back this
£10. Keep this document as part of your tax
records.

If you have to pay higher-rate tax, then you will have
to pay extra tax on the dividends you have received
in the tax year. Your gross dividend income will be
taxed at the rate of 32.5%. As you have already

paid 10%, you will owe a further 22.5% on the gross dividend, which is 25% of the net dividend. You can work out the gross amount of the dividend by adding up the amount you got and the tax credit. Even if you do not pay higher-rate tax, you may need to work out the grossed-up amount to see if you are entitled to the higher tax allowances for people aged 65 or more (see pages 7–10).

Unit trusts and OEICs

The income from unit trusts or Open Ended Investment Companies (OEICs) can be paid either as interest or as dividends. If it is paid as interest – often called an 'interest distribution' – it is treated like interest on money in a bank or building society. Tax will be deducted at 20% before you are paid the interest. If it is paid as a dividend, it is taxed like dividends.

ISAs and PEPs

Individual Savings Accounts (ISAs) were introduced in 1999 as a new way of tax-free saving. ISAs are not investments in themselves. They are simply a way of labelling savings or investments to show they are tax-free.

You can put up to £3,000 in cash into a cash ISA each tax year and another £4,000 into an ISA invested in shares or other things like bonds or gilts. Alternatively, you can put the whole £7,000 into investments – but not into cash. The interest earned is tax-free and no Capital Gains Tax is paid on any gain. If the money is invested in shares, then the automatic 10% tax is still taken off any dividends. So shares ISAs are really only any good for higher-rate taxpayers. The limits are changing in April 2008.

PEPs – Personal Equity Plans – were an earlier form of tax-free stock market investment. No new money could be put in them from April 1999 and they will be renamed ISAs in April 2008.

Other investment income

If you have purchased an annuity as an investment rather than as part of a pension plan, only part of the money you get each month is treated as income – the rest is treated as a return of your capital and is not taxed. The income part is normally paid with 20% tax automatically deducted.

If your income is below your tax allowances, or you are only due to pay tax at the 10% rate, you can claim back some or all of this tax. If you are due to pay tax at the higher rate, then you will have to pay extra tax on this income. Only the part treated as income is counted when you work out your entitlement to age-related tax allowances.

The Revenue says it is keen to help people claim back tax they may have overpaid on savings and investments. You can ring the Taxback Helpline on 0845 077 6543, or call 0845 980 0645 about registering to have your interest paid gross. Calls are charged at local rates. There is also a useful booklet, IR111 Bank and building society interest:

Are you paying tax when you don't need to?*, which is available from tax offices, the Orderline on 0845 900 0404 (calls are charged at local rates), or the Revenue website, which has a taxback section at www.hmrc.gov.uk/taxback*

What are tax codes?

A tax code normally consists of a number followed by a letter. The number represents the amount of money you can have tax-free in the year, with the last digit removed.

£ So if the tax allowance is £5,225, your code would start 522. Your employer then knows to allow you £5,229 during the year without taking any tax off.

The last figure is always a '9' to try to make sure the code system errs on your side: in other words, your allowance is slightly higher than the £5,225 it should be.

The number is followed by a letter that shows what kind of allowance you have. A common code for people under 65 is 522L. The 'L' stands for lower personal allowance – there isn't a lower personal allowance anymore but quite a lot of things in tax codes are hangovers from the past.

One thing that confuses people is that their State Pension is taxable – but it is paid in full without tax taken off. If you have other income from earnings or another pension, then the Revenue collects the tax due on it by deducting the amount of the State Pension from your tax allowance.

The common letters used in tax codes are:

- **L** – you get the personal allowance for people under 65.
- **P** – you get the full personal allowance for someone aged 65–74.
- **Y** – you get the full personal allowance for someone aged 75 or over.
- **V** – you are a basic-rate taxpayer and get both the personal allowance and Married Couple's Allowance for someone aged under 75, and pay basic-rate tax.

Irene *is 70 and has a State Pension of £90.50 a week, which is £4,706 a year. Irene's age is between 65 and 74, so her tax allowance is £7,550. She takes her State Pension from her allowance to give £2,844 and knocks off the last digit to give 284. She checks her code and sees it is 284P. The 'P' means she gets the full higher personal allowance for someone aged 65–74. The code means that this year she is allowed £2,849 on top of her State Pension before tax is due. So if her other income is £237 a month or less, then she will pay no tax on it.*

- **K** – if your pension is more than your tax allowance, then you will be given a K code. You get a K code when untaxed income, such as the State Pension or gross interest from savings, exceeds your personal allowances. The 'K' comes before the digits and means that you have a 'negative' allowance – in other words, instead of deducting an amount from your income before tax is worked out, extra income is added and tax worked out on the total. The amount to add is divided by 10 and rounded down to the nearest whole number and then placed after the K. That means the actual income you have is taxed at a higher rate than normal. But you will never have tax deducted at more than 50% from your income.

Myra *is 62. She has worked all her life and has paid full National Insurance contributions for most of that time. Her State Pension is now £133 a week (£6,916 a year). But as she is 62, her tax allowance is only £5,225. So she has to pay tax on £1,691 of her pension. As she is still in work that is done by adding that amount on to her earnings before the tax is worked out. The £1,691 is divided by ten and rounded down to 169 and her tax code is K169.*

Other codes you might see are:

- **T** – is used if your age-related personal allowance is reduced because your income is above the income limit of £20,900. You will also get a 'T' code if you have asked the tax office not to reveal to your employer or pension payer what your circumstances are.

- **0T** – is a variation of the T code and indicates that there is no tax allowance and all the income is to be taxed at the starting rate and the basic rate.

- **BR** – tax is to be collected at the basic rate on all of this source of income. This code might be used if you have more than one source of income. The tax allowance is normally included in the tax code for your main source of income and so tax is due on all other sources of income.

- **D0** – means all the income from this job or pension is to be taxed at the higher rate of 40%. That might happen if you had several sources of income which in total were well above £39,825 in 2007/08.

- **NT** – no tax is to be deducted – a rare but welcome code!

If you reach 65 or 75 during the tax year, then the Revenue will not include the higher tax allowance as part of your tax code automatically. That is not a mistake – it is a policy! The Revenue prefers to wait until the following tax year and then adjust that tax code to refund any tax overpaid. But if you insist it will change your tax code in good time.

Tax-saving tip: *If your 65th or 75th birthday is due in 2007/08, tell the Revenue now and say you want the correct allowance at once.*

Notice of Coding

The Revenue used to issue a Notice of Coding to everyone on PAYE each year. Employees now no longer get this service if their circumstances remain the same each year. But if you are on PAYE and you have a State Pension or other amounts deducted from your code, then you should get a Notice of Coding – called a P2 – each year, normally in January or February, so you can check it. It will show your tax code and how it is worked out.

The Revenue used to include with it a useful leaflet called *Understanding your tax code*. But it has stopped producing it – instead the Notice of Coding P2 should contain notes and information that explains how your tax code is worked out. It also tells you the tax office to contact if you think the coding is wrong.

 You can read more about tax codes on the Revenue website at www.hmrc.gov.uk/pensioners/understand ingyourp2.htm

If you have more than one source of income taxed through PAYE, you will have a tax code (and a Notice of Coding) for each. But your allowances will normally be used for the biggest source of income. The other sources may have a 0T, BR or D0 code. Check that the figures are correct and that the calculation makes sense.

When you get a new Notice of Coding, check that:
- you have been given the correct allowances – on at least one of your income sources;
- the deductions for the State Pension and any untaxed investment income are correct;
- the addition and subtraction are right; and

- the code letter is the appropriate one for your circumstances.

If you disagree with anything on the Notice of Coding, take a copy of it and send the original back to the tax office, saying what you think is wrong. Alternatively, you can phone your tax office to find out more or to request that a change should be made.

Code changes

There may be changes in your circumstances that affect your code. For example:

- **If you get a new source of income** – perhaps you start a new job or self-employment, or you start drawing a pension – then your tax code may not cope with the change. If you change jobs, the employer you leave should give you a form for your new employer called a P45, which shows your tax code. Until they get that P45 your earnings will normally be taxed on an 'emergency code'. That may mean you pay too much tax.

- **In some circumstances you will start a job and not have a P45** – that might happen if you retired from a job, got an occupational pension, and then took up a new job. If you do not have a P45, your new employer should ask you to sign form P46 and give you form P15 (allowances claim) so that the right PAYE code can be obtained for taxing your earnings.

It is up to you to inform the tax office of any changes that might affect your code and the amount of tax you pay. But even if you do not, remember that the code is only a way of collecting the tax, *not* of assessing it. If you end up paying too much, you can claim it back – and if you pay too little, the Revenue can demand it from you later.

If your code does change – apart from the change when the personal allowance goes up each year – you should be notified by the Revenue. If the number in the code goes up, you will be paying less tax through PAYE; if it goes down, you will be paying more – it's the opposite way round with the K code of course.

What can go wrong?

The simple answer to that question is – lots of things. Here are just some of the things that can go wrong that help the Revenue deduct £500 million too much each year:

- **The amount of your State Pension changes in April** and the Department for Work and Pensions (DWP) should automatically provide information to the Revenue about how much it is. Sometimes, though, the two government departments cannot match up the data and the Revenue is not told exactly how much your pension is. In that case it will work out your new pension from last year's figure. But that calculation is approximate and may be wrong. So always check that the correct amount of pension has been taken into account. If the amount of your State Pension has been overestimated, contact your tax office to explain; otherwise you will pay too much tax.

- **If you have any untaxed investment income** – such as the interest on government stock (gilts – see page 27) or from offshore savings – then an estimated amount for that may be deducted from your allowance. The deduction will be slightly less than the amount of the interest. That is so the extra tax – which is calculated at 22% – equals the tax that should be taken at 20%. Remember this is an estimate. If the actual amount is different, then the wrong tax will have been deducted throughout the year. So always check.

> **Ross** *has some government stock which earned him £400 last year in interest. He has to pay tax at 20% on that, which is £80. So the Revenue reduces his tax code by 36. That increases the tax he pays on his other income by £360 x 22%, which is £79.20. That almost covers the £80 and the Revenue will normally ignore the rest.*

- **Married Couple's Allowance** is a fixed amount deducted from your Income Tax, rather than being an allowance in the normal sense, and it cannot easily be taken account of in a tax code. But the Revenue tries to do just that. If you get Married Couple's Allowance, it will be added to your allowances but then an amount will be taken off it – called an allowance restriction – to try to make sure the tax is right. But it may give the wrong answer and you should check at the end of the tax year to see if the correct tax has been deducted. In some cases the Revenue does not impose the restriction and that can lead to too little tax being paid.

A useful leaflet explaining the restriction is no longer published by the Revenue. But you may find an old version for 2002 on its website.

If you get the Married Couple's Allowance and your spouse dies, or you stop living together permanently or divorce (or dissolve a civil partnership), then the allowance will normally cease from the following tax year. Make sure that is reflected in your code or you may end up paying too little tax.

How does self-assessment work?

More than a million pensioners pay their tax through the system called self-assessment. If you are one of them in 2007/08, you should have been sent a tax return in April 2007. This form relates to your income and allowances for 2006/07.

If you can, it is better to fill in the form and return it by 30 September 2007. The Revenue will then work out the tax you have to pay. If you delay beyond 30 September, the Revenue will not guarantee to do the calculation in time and you will have to work out the tax due. The absolute deadline for returning the form is 31 January 2008.

If you have to pay tax for 2006/07 it will be due on 31 January 2008. You may also have to make payments on account for 2007/08 (see page 46). If you miss these deadlines, you may be subject to penalties and interest.

Tax-saving tip: *When the self-assessment form arrives, check that it contains all the parts you need, return it by the deadline, and pay the tax when it is due.*

Who does it affect?

Most older people do not need to worry about self-assessment. But it may affect you if:

- you are self-employed, a partner in a business or a company director;
- you pay higher-rate tax;
- you are a minister of religion;
- your income is above £20,900;
- your only income is the State Pension and interest that is not taxed at source;
- you have untaxed income from investments (though if you are old enough to get State Pension and this can be collected through PAYE, then you will need to fill in a different form called P810); or
- you have rental income from letting a property outside the rent-a-room scheme.

Most older people who pay tax on their pension or earnings through PAYE, and whose savings interest has tax deducted from it before it is paid, will not be sent a tax return and need not worry about self-assessment.

But even if your income is quite low, you may still be sent a tax return if you have untaxed income that cannot be collected through PAYE.

If you have less than £2,500 of income that is not taxed at source and you have a PAYE code, then the tax will automatically be collected by adjusting your code.

You can opt out of this system by filling in a box – this year 23.1A – on your self-assessment return.

Filling in the form

The self-assessment tax returns are sent out after 5 April and ask for information about your income in the previous tax year. Along with the basic tax form, you may receive one or more supplementary pages covering sources of income such as employment, self-employment, or rental income. There may also be a guide to completing the form, and a separate booklet for the tax calculation. The forms are long and can seem very complicated, so allow yourself plenty of time and ask for help if necessary.

You may be able to get help from a local advice agency and there are three charities that will give you free help with tax. They are listed on page 110. Alternatively, you can ask the Revenue or pay an accountant or tax adviser to help you.

About one in three older people who have to fill in a self-assessment form will be sent a simpler four-page version called the Short Tax Return. You cannot apply to have the short form – if you get the long one, you must complete it – and if you are sent the short one, you have to check that you are eligible for it. Although the form is short, it comes with a 24-page guide. The first two pages help you to decide whether or not the form is suitable for you. The short form does not allow you to work out precisely how much tax you owe. So it really should be filled in and sent back by 30 September so that the Revenue can work things out in time for you to pay the correct amount of tax by 31 January 2008.

You can avoid a lot of trouble by using the Revenue's online self-assessment form. It is safe and secure. It works out the tax you owe, and you get a receipt for the form once you have submitted it. (If you post the paper form or deliver it personally to a local Revenue office, you do not get a receipt.)

You have to register first at https://online.inlandrevenue.gov.uk

The Revenue wants everyone to use the online service, and new rules and filing dates will apply for 2007/08 returns. You will have to file a paper form by 31 October 2008 (instead of 31 January 2009) or pay a penalty, but if you file online you can still wait until 31 January 2009. So if you can, it is worth changing this year.

If you are not usually sent a tax return but have a new source of income or a capital gain on which you need to pay tax, you must tell the Revenue by 5 October after the end of the tax year – so if you had a new source of income in 2006/07, you must tell the Revenue by 5 October 2007. You will then be sent a tax return to complete. Check when it has to be returned by.

When is tax paid?

Income Tax is charged on income received in the current tax year. The tax is due on 31 January and 31 July, with any balance due the following 31 January. In other words, at the end of January 2008 you are expected to pay half the tax due on income from 6 April 2007 to 5 April 2008. That is clearly impossible to do accurately, as you may not know exactly how much your income will be between 1 February and 5 April. So the tax you pay is always an estimate and the payments you make are called 'on account'. (No payment on account has to be made if the tax due is less than £500.) The tax paid is corrected in the following year from the information in your next tax return.

The timetable runs like this:

- **April 2007** – tax returns are sent out for the tax year 2006/07. You complete yours with the details of your income and allowances for 2006/07. That information is used to calculate exactly the tax that was due in 2006/07. You may have already made payments of this tax in January and July 2006.

- **30 September 2007** – if you send the form back by this date, the Revenue will calculate the tax due in 2006/07 and the estimated amount of the tax due in 2007/08 in time for the 31 January 2008 payment. Even if your return is in later than

30 September, the Revenue will still calculate the tax but may not do so in time for the January deadline – in which case, you have to work this out yourself.

- **31 January 2008** – half the estimated tax for 2007/08 is due (this is called a payment on account). In addition, any overpayment or underpayment for 2006/07 is corrected. If there was an underpayment, a further payment is due. If there has been an overpayment, then a refund is due. Normally, the extra money or the refund is simply added on or taken off the tax due on account for 2007/08.

If the balancing payment for 2006/07 is less than £2,000, it can be collected through PAYE in a future year, but only if you get your tax return back by 30 September 2007. If your income goes down significantly from one year to the next, then your estimated tax is likely to be more than the amount actually due. If your circumstances change in this way, you can tell the Revenue and pay less on account.

Ask for a form SA303 or download it at www.hmrc.gov.uk/sa/forms/sa303.pdf

But if it turns out you got it wrong and you pay too little tax, you will be charged interest on the unpaid tax back to the date it was due.

What records have to be kept?

All taxpayers are obliged by law to keep records of their income and capital gains. Unless you are self-employed (see pages 74–84) or rent out property (except under the rent-a-room scheme – see page 4), you can normally destroy records for 2005/06 – in other words, those relating to your affairs up to 5 April 2006 – on 1 February 2008. You may have to keep your records longer if:

- the tax return was late;
- there is an enquiry going on into your tax affairs; or
- your tax return was sent to you late in the year.

If you are self-employed or have rental income, the deadline for destroying documents is normally five years later (see pages 81–82).

What penalties are there?

If you are sent a form, you must complete it. If you do not, you could face a penalty. If you want the Revenue to do the calculation, send back the form by 30 September 2007; if you miss that deadline, there are no penalties but you may have to calculate the tax yourself and get the form in by 31 January 2008. If you miss the January deadline, you will be fined; and if you pay the tax after that date, you may incur interest and surcharges on any tax paid late.

The key dates for tax returns for 2006/07 are:

- **April 2007** – tax returns for 2006/07 are sent out by the Revenue to people it thinks need to fill one in.

- **30 September 2007** – if you do not return your form by this date, the Revenue will not guarantee to calculate your tax by the time it is due. If your form misses this date, you will not be able to arrange to pay extra tax due through the PAYE system.

- **31 January 2008** – you must send back your tax return by this date. The penalty for missing this date is normally £100 (but if you owe less tax than £100, the penalty cannot be more than the tax that is due). If you do not owe any tax or you have a reasonable excuse for your return being late, you will not have to pay the penalty. Some people are sent penalties by mistake. So always consider appealing against a penalty. There may also be a daily fine of £60 for each day the form is late but this is rarely imposed.

- **31 January 2008** – a balancing payment for 2006/07 is due, and so is the payment on account for the tax year 2007/08. Penalty interest is charged on unpaid tax for every day it is late. From August 2007 this rate is 8.5% a year.

- **28 February 2008** – a 5% surcharge is added onto any tax due for 2006/07 that has still not been paid.

- **28 March 2008** – if the surcharge has not been paid, interest begins to be charged on the surcharge.

- **31 July 2008** – if your tax return has still not been submitted, a second £100 penalty is imposed.

- **31 July 2008** – a further 5% surcharge is added to any tax due for 2006/07 that has still not been paid.

- **28 August 2008** – if the further surcharge has not been paid, interest begins to be charged on it.

For further information, help or leaflets, contact the Self-Assessment Team at your tax office (the telephone number is at the top of your return). In the evenings and at weekends you can call the Revenue's Self-Assessment Helpline on 0845 9000 444. Or check out the website at www.hmrc.gov.uk/sa/forms/content.htm

After you send in your tax return

If you have asked the Revenue to calculate your tax bill, or you have calculated your tax but the Revenue has changed your figures, you will be sent a Tax Calculation. You should check that the figures are correct and that you agree with any changes made. If you want to amend anything, let the Revenue know as soon as possible.

Everyone who is sent a tax return has a 'tax account' opened at the Revenue. You will receive a Statement of Account once a year showing the money you owe. You will also receive one in certain other circumstances, including:

- when there are changes to items in your account;
- when a tax payment is due in the next 35 days;
- every two months when between £32 and £500 is due;
- every month when over £500 is due;
- when the Revenue has arranged for unpaid tax to be collected through PAYE; or
- when you have paid more tax than is due.

Check your Statement of Account when you receive it, and contact the Revenue if you disagree with the entries. A small number of tax returns are selected for investigation – they are called 'enquiries'. Usually this is because something appears wrong or if the figures have changed significantly from one year to the next. But a few tax returns are selected at random.

Tax-saving tip: *Even if you get your form in by 30 September and the Revenue works out your tax, check it. The Revenue admits that it gets around half a million self-assessment calculations wrong each year. You can claim back any tax that has been overpaid.*

Who has to pay National Insurance contributions?

If you work and earn £100 a week or more, you will have to pay National Insurance contributions. They will normally be deducted from your pay before you get it. But these contributions stop in the week you reach State Pension age – currently 60 for a woman, 65 for a man.

Tax-saving tip: *Once you reach 60 or 65, check that no National Insurance contributions are being deducted from your pay. They should stop with the last payment before your birthday.*

If you are self-employed and are below State Pension age, then you may have to pay two separate National Insurance contributions – they are called Class 2 and Class 4:

- **Class 2 contributions** are £2.20 a week in the 2007/08 tax year. If you reach State Pension age during a tax year, you can stop paying Class 2 in the week you reach that age. Class 2 contributions are paid quarterly, or when you are sent a bill, or by monthly direct debit. Revenue leaflet SE1 includes a direct-debit mandate you can use. You will be exempt from Class 2 contributions if you expect your annual profit to be below £4,635. But you must claim this exemption in advance.

Download the form at www.hmrc.gov.uk/leaflets/se1.pdf and send it off as soon as you can.

In practice the Revenue may agree to backdate an application. Class 2 contributions count towards your State Pension.

- **Class 4 contributions** are collected by the Revenue with your Income Tax. Contributions are charged at 8% on profits between £5,225 and £34,840 in 2007/08 and at 1% on income above that. You have to pay Class 4 contributions for the whole tax year in which you reach State Pension age, but not after that. Class 4 contributions do not help you qualify for a State Pension or other benefits. They are simply a tax.

If you have income from paid employment as well as from self-employment, and you are under State Pension age, you will be paying **Class 1 contributions**, which are deducted straight from your earnings.

There are complex rules that fix a maximum amount of National Insurance contributions you have to pay, and your Class 2 and Class 4 contributions may be reduced. If this is likely to apply to you, seek advice from NICO.

Tax-saving tip: *If you are employed and self-employed, check that you are not paying too much in National Insurance contributions.*

For more information, see the Revenue website at www.hmrc.gov.uk/nic/class2.htm and www.hmrc.gov.uk/nic/class4.htm

Married women's reduced-rate contributions

It is not often that this book recommends paying *more* tax. But one group of working women should consider doing so. If you are under 60, married and have been in work fairly continuously since before May 1977, then you may still be paying the reduced-rate married women's National Insurance Contributions.

These contributions earn you nothing. They do *not* count towards a State Pension. They are a complete waste of money.

Unfortunately, the only way to stop paying them is to change to the full contributions. That will cost you more but they earn you rights to the State Pension *and* count towards the earnings-related State Second Pension (which used to be called SERPS). For most women aged under 59 it is better to change. You can do that at any time during the tax year on form CF9. The only group who may gain nothing from changing at the moment are those who pay into salary-related company pension schemes and who have a very small entitlement to their own State Pension.

For more information see www.hmrc.gov.uk/faqs/women_reduced_ rate.htm and for the form to fill in see www.hmrc.gov.uk/forms/cf9.pdf

Overpaid contributions

If you have paid too much in National Insurance contributions, you can claim the excess back. There are several reasons why you might pay too much – for example:

- you stopped being self-employed;
- you were working or self-employed after reaching State Pension age;
- your earnings were below £100 a week;
- you had more than one job;
- you were employed and self-employed at the same time; or
- you qualified for small earnings exception but did not apply.

Most overpaid National Insurance contributions can only be reclaimed for the last six years. But if you paid too much in contributions because you have more than one job or you earned below the threshold and should not have paid contributions at all, you can reclaim the overpayment without any time limit.

If you think you have overpaid, apply in writing to HM Revenue & Customs, NICO, Benton Park View, Newcastle upon Tyne NE98 1ZZ. Send them any evidence you have and explain which contributions you think you have overpaid. Always include your National Insurance number.

How to check your tax bill

Even the Revenue admits that many people pay too much or too little tax. PAYE, self-assessment, and the automatic deduction of tax from interest, are all responsible for the wrong tax being deducted. People with more than once source of income, and people who reach 65 or 75 during the tax year, are also often charged the wrong tax.

This section of the book shows you how to check that you are paying the right amount of Income Tax. If you follow the steps below, you should be able to see whether you should pay tax and how much you are due to pay. It is complicated and you will need a calculator, paper and pen, and a logical approach.

Your income comes in two sorts and each sort is taxed differently. First, there is income from investments – that is like the cream and always sits on the top of your income. At the very top of the cream is the double cream of your dividends. Second, sitting under the cream, is the milk of all your other income. Generally, tax allowances and rates of tax are applied from the bottom of these layers up. So the allowances or the tax applies first to your non-investment income and then to interest and income from investments, and finally to dividends.

Step 1

- £ List your income separately in two columns – investment income in Column A, and all the rest (such as pensions and earnings – and rent, apart from the rent-a-room scheme) in Column B.
- £ Delete all the income that is tax-free (see pages 2–6).
- £ Make sure that all the remaining income is listed gross (in other words, before tax is deducted). For income that you receive tax-paid, such as interest on money in a bank or building society, gross it up by dividing by 4 and multiplying by 5. If you have dividend income, divide it by 9 and multiply by 10.
- £ Add up each Column (A and B) separately to get Total A and Total B.
- £ Then add them together to get your 'total income'.

Step 2

- £ Look up your personal allowance on page 104. If you are aged 65 or over and your total income is less than £20,900, you can claim the full personal allowance for your age.

£ If it is more than £20,900, reduce the allowance by £1 for every £2 above £20,900. But do not reduce your personal allowance below £5,225.

£ If you are blind, add on the £1,730 Blind Person's Allowance too.

£ Don't add on the Married Couple's Allowance even if you are entitled to it. It is dealt with at step 6. (Allowances and how to work out your total income are explained on pages 7–12.)

Step 3

£ If your tax allowance is more than your total income, then *no tax is due*. Stop now!

£ Subtract your allowance from your total income. If the answer is less than £2,230, then your tax is just 10% of the answer. Skip steps 4 and 5 and go straight to step 6.

£ Otherwise, separate out your income into the two columns A (interest and dividends) and B (other income).

£ If the allowance is less than the amount in Column B, subtract the allowance from the Column B income and write down the result. Then go straight to step 4.

£ If the allowance is more than the amount in Column B, then subtract the total in Column B from the allowance and subtract that answer from the total in Column A. Skip step 4 and go straight to step 5.

Step 4

- £ The first £2,230 of your income above the allowances is taxed at 10%. So write down £223.

- £ The other income above that up to £32,370 (£34,600 – £2,230) is taxed at 22%. Multiply the amount by 0.22 and write that down.

- £ If there is more income above that, it is taxed at 40%. So multiply the excess by 0.4 and write it down.

- £ When you run out of income from Column B, look at your income in Column A (interest).

- £ If you have identified any income to be taxed at 40%, then tax the savings income at 40% and the dividend income at 22.5%.

- £ Otherwise, ignore the dividend income, and tax the rest at 20%. Add up the amounts of tax due. Skip step 5 and go to step 6.

Step 5

You reached this step because your tax-free allowance used up all your 'other' Column B income. You should have deducted the balance of your allowance from your investment income in Column A.

- £ Now deduct any income from dividends.

- £ The first £2,230 of your remaining investment is taxed at 10%. If there is other income left above that, the next slice up to £32,370 above the £2,230 is taxed at 20%. If there is more above that, it is taxed at 40%. If you have identified any income to be taxed at 40%, then tax your gross dividends at 22.5% – otherwise do not tax them at all.

£ Add up the amounts of tax due.

Step 6

£ If you qualify for a Married Couple's Allowance (one of you must have been born before 6 April 1935), look up the value of your allowance in the table on pages 104–105.

£ If this is more than the tax you are due to pay, that wipes out your tax liability and you have no tax to pay.

£ Otherwise, deduct the amount from the tax you are due to pay.

£ The balance is the tax you should pay altogether in 2007/08. Much or all of this tax will already have been paid either through PAYE or through the automatic deduction of tax from investment income.

Step 7

£ Add up the tax that has already been deducted from the interest paid on a bank or building society account.

£ Deduct that total from the tax you are due to pay.

£ If it is bigger than the tax you are due to pay, then you may be due some tax back. Apply for a refund.

£ If it is smaller, this is the amount of tax you still have to pay. Check how much tax has been deducted through PAYE. If it is more than the tax due, apply for a refund.

Examples

1. Single person

Joan, 77, gets the Basic State Pension, which includes some Graduated Retirement Benefit and totals £92.05 a week. She also has a small pension from her former employer of £151 a month gross. She checks her building society account and finds that the interest earned was £424 over the year and she grosses that up by multiplying by 5 and dividing by 4, which is £530 gross and she has had £106 deducted in tax.

Joan follows the steps set out above to work out her tax for the 2007/08 tax year:

Step 1: She writes down all her income, remembering to use the gross amount of her building society interest, and adds it up:

State Pension	£4,786.60
Pension from employer	£1,812.00
Interest on savings (gross)	£530.00
Total income	**£7,128.60**

Step 2: As Joan is over 75, she is entitled to the highest level of personal allowance. As her total income is less than £20,900, she can claim the full higher allowance of £7,690 for someone over 75.

Step 3: Joan's income of £7,128.60 is less than her personal allowance of £7,690, so no tax is due. But Joan has had £106 deducted from her building society interest. She checks back and finds that this has happened every year. So she claims back the overpaid tax, on Form R40, back to 2001/02 (it comes to more than £400). She also fills in form R85 so that in future her interest is paid gross.

Tax-saving tip: *If you are not liable to pay tax, make sure you do not have tax deducted from interest on your savings in a bank or building society account.*

2. Married couple – both pay tax

Ravi is 73 and married to **Sangeeta**, who is 63. They must look at their tax positions separately.

Ravi: He has retired and receives a State Pension of £111.90 a week, which includes some SERPS (officially called Additional Pension) from a previous job. He also receives an occupational pension from his last employer of £585 a month gross. He and Sangeeta have a joint building society account on which they received net interest of £504. The Revenue will treat this as being split equally between them – £252 each. That is grossed up as £252 x 5 ÷ 4 = £315.

Step 1: Ravi works out his total income for 2007/08:

State Pension	£5,818.80
Pension from employer	£7,020.00
Half interest on savings, grossed up	£315.00
Total income	**£13,153.80**

Step 2: Ravi is entitled to a personal allowance for someone aged 65–74. As his total income is below £20,900, he gets the full allowance for people aged 65–74, which is £7,550.

Step 3: Ravi's income is more than his personal allowance, so some tax is due. He separates his income into savings and other income and deducts the personal allowance of £7,550 from his other income of £12,838.80 – without his interest – which leaves £5,288.80.

Step 4: Ravi works out the tax due in this step:

10% of the first £2,230	£223.00
22% of the remaining £3,058.80	£672.94
20% of his £315 gross savings income	£63.00
Total tax due in this step	**£958.94**

Step 5: He skips this step.

Step 6: Ravi is 73 in July 2007, so he was born before 6 April 1935, and can get the Married Couple's Allowance, which at his age is £6,285. So his tax bill is reduced by 10% of that (£628.50). He deducts this from the tax due in step 4 of £958.94 – £628.50 = £330.44. So that amount is the tax he should have paid.

He has already paid his share of the tax on his building society account, which amounts to £63, so he should only have tax of £330.44 – £63.00 = £267.44 deducted from his pension, at the rate of £22.29 a month. When he checks, he finds that he has had more than this deducted, so he claims a refund.

Sangeeta then does her tax: She has recently retired from full-time work but does not get a pension from her former employer. She gets the married woman's pension of £52.30 a week, paid as a result of Ravi's contributions. She is still working part-time, 15 hours a week at £5.60 an hour, which is £84 a week. And she has her share of the interest on their joint savings – £315 gross.

Step 1: She adds up her income:

State Pension	£2,719.60
Earnings	£4,368.00
Half interest on savings, grossed up	£315.00
Total income	**£7,402.60**

Step 2: Sangeeta is under 65, so she is only entitled to the basic personal allowance of £5,225.

Step 3: Sangeeta's total taxable income is more than her personal allowance, so tax is due. The difference is only £2,177.60, which is less than £2,230. So she taxes the £2,177.60 at 10%. Sangeeta's tax so far is: 10% of £2,177.60 = £217.76. She skips to:

Step 6: She is not entitled to a Married Couple's Allowance – Ravi has that and she does not need any of it transferred to her. She checks her wages and finds that over the year she has paid £186.26 in tax. She has also had tax at 20% deducted automatically from her interest. Her share of that is £63.

Altogether she has paid £249.26 tax (£31.50 too much as her tax due is £217.76). So she claims £31.50 back from the Revenue. She finds her local Tax Enquiry Centre in the phone book and gets form R40, fills it in, and sends it off. She is delighted to find that she also gets some money back for previous years too.

Tax-saving tip: *If you are only due to pay tax at 10%, then you can claim back half the tax the bank or building society has deducted from your interest.*

3. Couple where one partner pays no tax

Sid is 69 and his wife **Lillian** is 67. In 2007/08 Sid receives the State Pension, which in his case is £94 a week, and a pension from his job of £1,290 a month. Sid also put a lump sum in the building society when he retired and that brought in £1,300 in 2007/08, which he and Lillian found very useful. Sid grosses it up, which means he counts £1,625 as his income.

Lillian gets the married woman's pension of £52.30 a week on Sid's contributions but she does get a bit extra amounting to £2.74 a week – a total of £2,862.08 a year. This is much less than her personal allowance of £7,550, so she should pay no tax. Sid, however, pays quite a lot.

Step 1: Sid adds up his total income:

State Pension	£4,888
Occupational pension	£15,480
Building society interest (gross)	£1,625
Total income	**£21,993**

Step 2: Sid is 69 and so he should be entitled to the higher personal allowance of £7,550. But Sid's gross income of £21,993 is more than the income limit of £20,900 for the higher levels of personal allowance. He takes one from the other and gets £1,093, so he halves that (see pages 9–10), and deducts the £546 from his

maximum personal allowance of £7,550 to get £7,004, which is his personal allowance for 2007/08.

Step 3: Sid has to pay tax and he has to pay it on more than £2,230, so he subtracts his personal allowance of £7,004 from his 'other' income (£4,888 + £15,480 = £20,368 – £7,004 = £13,364).

Step 4: The first £2,230 is taxed at 10% and the rest is taxed at 22%. His savings income is taxed at 20%:

10% of the first £2,230 taxable income	£223.00
22% of the remaining £11,134	£2,449.48
20% of interest of £1,625	£325.00
Total tax bill	**£2,997.48**

Step 6: Sid skips step 5 and comes to step 6. Sid's Married Couple's Allowance is £6,285 and the value is £628.50. He deducts that from his tax. Total tax due is £2,997.48 – £628.50 = £2,368.98.

Step 7: Sid checks his tax and finds he has paid tax on his savings through the automatic deduction by the building society. Tax on his State Pension and his occupational pension was deducted through PAYE from his occupational pension. He finds it is not quite right – he actually has not paid quite enough tax because the coding could not cope with the reduction in his personal allowance.

Sid tells the tax office but is advised that he could actually pay less tax if he transferred the money in his building society account to Lillian. If he had done so before the start of the tax year, Lillian's income this tax year would then have consisted of the State Pension of £2,862.08 plus the interest of £1,625. This total of £4,487.08 would still be well below her personal allowance of £7,550 and so no tax would be due on it. As a non-taxpayer she could have applied to have the interest paid without the tax being deducted. That would have saved them the £325 tax due on the interest.

But the savings don't stop there. Sid's total income would then have been £20,368, which is just below £20,900 limit for the age allowance. So he would get the higher personal allowance in full of £7,550. That would have cut his tax bill by a further £120.12, so altogether he could have saved £445.12, which is more than £8.50 a week. Sid makes the change at once and, although the savings are not quite so great this year, they have a holiday on the proceeds. Next year they will save the full amount.

Tax-saving tip: *If one partner pays no tax or tax at a lower rate, you can save tax by transferring income or savings to that partner.*

Before you do this, remember that, although transferring assets can save tax, there can also be disadvantages. For example, if Sid gave all his savings to Lillian and then she had to go into a care home, those savings would mean she got no help with her fees. If you do transfer assets, this must be a genuine gift, so the recipient has complete control over the asset – you must not keep an interest in it yourself.

Conclusion

Phew! Well done for getting to the end of the chapter. Finally, remember two things. The Revenue makes lots of mistakes. So always check what it tells you. If you come up with a different answer or you just do not understand something, don't be embarrassed to ask the Revenue to explain its calculations. Second, the rules about paying tax are deeply biased in favour of the Revenue. If you make a mistake or miss a payment, you can be penalised or fined. If the Revenue makes a mistake or misses a deadline, the closest you get to an apology will usually be a shrug. So err on the side of caution and claim it back later.

Dealing with the Revenue

HM Revenue & Customs (HMRC) is the government department that deals with almost all the taxes due in the UK. Which tax office handles your affairs will depend on your circumstances:

- if you are still in paid work, it will be your employer's tax office;
- if you are self-employed, it will usually be the office covering the location of your business (that could be in a completely different part of the country);
- if you are unemployed or retired, it may be your last employer's tax office; or
- if you are receiving a pension or annuity, it will usually be the office dealing with the pension provider.

If you have more than one source of income, then more than one tax office may be involved. But there will always be one main office that should co-ordinate your tax affairs.

It's likely that your tax office will not be nearby, so you will have to contact it by letter or phone. When writing, always include your tax reference number or your National Insurance number, which you will find on papers you have received from the

Revenue. Keep correspondence you receive, and always take a copy of letters and papers you send.

Contacting your tax office by phone may be quicker and easier, though, and if you are worried about the cost you can ask to be rung back. Take notes during a telephone conversation; it is sensible to follow it up afterwards with a letter to confirm what was said. Ask the tax office to do the same.

 You can make general enquiries at your local tax office (look in the business section of the phone book under HM Revenue & Customs). You will need to make an appointment – the walk-in Tax Enquiry Centres have now all closed.

Claiming tax back

If you think you may have paid too much tax, you can claim it back. Write to your tax office setting out why you think you have overpaid and by how much. You can claim for the current year 2007/08 and up to six years back – right back to 2001/02. If the Revenue made a mistake, you may be able to go back even further. And you may get interest – currently 4% – on overpaid tax.

Underpayment of tax

If you have not paid enough tax in the current tax year or in previous years, then you will owe tax and have to pay it. There may also be interest to pay – currently at 8.5% – and there may be penalties if the Revenue thinks you have not been cooperative.

It is easy to pay too little tax by mistake. Many older people whose tax affairs are straightforward do not receive a tax return every year. So if you have recently started to receive income from a new source, such as savings or investments, the Revenue may not be aware of it. If you think you may have income that you have not reported, contact your tax office and explain.

Normally, you have to tell the Revenue about any new source of income by 5 October in the tax year after it is received. So if you have new income in the tax year 2007/08, you must tell the Revenue by 5 October 2008. The Revenue can go back for up to six tax years, or longer in the case of negligence or fraud, to examine your income and the tax due.

People who have deliberately evaded tax or who have seriously neglected their tax affairs may be liable to penalties of up to the same amount as the tax due. In the very rare cases where fraud has been committed the Revenue may bring criminal proceedings.

Tax-saving tip: *If the Revenue charges you penalties on underpaid tax, always put in an appeal against them. Penalties can be withdrawn if you made a genuine mistake and can show that you have cooperated fully.*

Official delays

If the Revenue has been very slow in dealing with your tax affairs or in taking into account information it has been given, and it later discovers that you have not paid enough tax, you may not have to pay the difference. You could qualify for what is known as 'Extra-Statutory Concession A19'. This concession applies if:

- the Revenue fails to act on information supplied by you, your employer, or the Department for Work and Pensions; and
- you could reasonably have believed that your tax affairs were in order.

But the concession is not normally given if you were notified of the arrears in the tax year in which they arose or by the end of the following tax year.

Getting help and advice

If you need help with your tax affairs, you can get help or information at a Revenue Local Enquiry Centre but you will have to make an appointment. That may be easier than contacting your own tax office as it will probably be closer, so you could talk to someone face to face. If you cannot get out, the Centre may be able to arrange a home visit. If you have hearing difficulties, the Revenue can provide services such as Textphone and Typetalk, although not all offices have these.

 The Revenue produces a number of leaflets about tax but most of them are now only available online (from www.hmrc.gov.uk). The few that are still printed can be obtained from a local HMRC office. Some can be provided in Braille, audio or large print on request. You can also get them through the Orderline on 08459 000 404 (calls are charged at local rates).

If your tax position is complicated, perhaps because you are self-employed or have considerable investment income, you will probably need to employ an accountant or tax adviser.

There are three free and independent tax advice services for older people who cannot afford an accountant or tax adviser – see page 110.

Appeals and complaints

If you disagree with a decision about your tax, you can appeal against it. For example, you may think you have been incorrectly charged a late-filing penalty on your tax return.

You appeal by writing to the Inspector of Taxes at your tax office. You should do this within 30 days of receiving the decision you disagree with.

Often appeals are settled by agreement, but you have the right to take a case to an independent tribunal. This is intended to be an informal process and you cannot be asked to pay costs.

Further information is given in the Department for Constitutional Affairs leaflet Tax appeals, *which is available from your tax office or online at www.hmrc.gov.uk/leaflets/tax-appeals.pdf*

The Revenue sets strict standards for how it deals with customers, even if sometimes they seem to be more about how long it takes to respond rather than whether the answer was clear.

*These standards are set down in leaflet
COP10 (see
www.hmrc.gov.uk/pdfs/cop10.htm) and
the online leaflet C/FS sets out what to
do if you have a complaint (see
www.hmrc.gov.uk/factsheets/complaints-
factsheet.pdf).*

If the Revenue does make a mistake that causes
you expense, you can reclaim this money. You
may also get a payment of between £25 and £500
to compensate you for distress and
inconvenience. If you have spent money making
the complaint, then you can also reclaim those
costs as long as they are reasonable.

If you are not satisfied with the Revenue's
response to a complaint, there is an Adjudicator's
Office that can consider the matter and
recommend appropriate action. The Adjudicator is
independent of the Revenue. If your problem has
been caused by maladministration, you can refer a
complaint to the Parliamentary Ombudsman
through your MP.

For further information, see leaflet AO1,
The Adjudicator's Office for Complaints
about HM Revenue & Customs and the
Valuation Office Agency. *You can get a
copy from any tax office, or by phoning
the Adjudicator's Office on 020 7930
2292, or from the website at
www.adjudicatorsoffice.gov.uk/pdf/ao1.pdf*

Self-employment

Many people can become self-employed in retirement without realising it. For example, you may in fact be self-employed if you:

- buy things to sell at car boot sales or on eBay:
- write the odd article for money;
- become a local handyman for neighbours who pay you; or
- do regular babysitting for money.

There is no minimum amount of earnings before you become self-employed. Strictly speaking, if you do any work or trading for money on your own account you are self-employed. And although your earnings may be too low to pay tax or National Insurance, you still count as self-employed.

If you are self-employed, you will have to fill in a self-assessment form and have to work out your own profits and pay your own Income Tax. If your turnover is less than £15,000 the details required on the form are very few.

If you are under State Pension age, you may also have to pay your own National Insurance contributions (NICs: see pages 51–55).

If your annual turnover is more than £64,000, you may also have to charge Value Added Tax (VAT) on your invoices and pay that to the

Revenue. If your turnover is less than £150,000, you may benefit from the flat-rate scheme (see page 84).

Income from self-employment is added to income from pensions and other sources to determine the total amount of tax you are liable to pay. You will have income from self-employment if you are in business on your own account, even on a part-time or occasional basis, provided that the money you earn exceeds your business expenses.

Further details are given in the Revenue leaflet SE1, Thinking of working for yourself? *There is also a yellow link on the front page of the Revenue website about self-employment (www.hmrc.gov.uk). You can also find out more from* The No-nonsense guide to government rules and regulations for setting up your business, *which is also published by the Government. You can download a copy from the website at http://tinyurl.com/a778q or get a copy by calling 0845 600 9 006.*

Notifying the Revenue

If you become self-employed, you are legally obliged to notify the Revenue when you start. Registration is required for both Income Tax and National Insurance and you can register for both at the same time.

If you don't register within the first three full months of self-employment, you may be liable for a penalty of £100. If you have still not registered by 6 October following the end of the tax year in which you started up, further penalties may be due. You must register even if you earn very little, or even nothing, from your self-employment.

You can notify the Revenue that you are self-employed simply by writing to your local tax office. Always keep a copy of any letter you send. A better method may be to obtain leaflet SE1 and fill in form CWF1, which it contains. You can also register by phone – call the Revenue helpline for the newly self-employed on 08459 15 45 15.

Your accounting date

Once the Revenue knows you are self-employed, you should be sent a self-assessment form each April, including the pages for self-employment. If your turnover is less than £15,000, you will normally be sent the Short Tax Return, which is easier to fill in. On this you must declare your business income and expenses. The balance of your income, less your expenses, is your taxable profit – in other words, it is the income on which you are liable to pay tax.

Although the Income Tax year runs from 6 April to the following 5 April, you can fix your own 'accounting year' over which you work out your income and expenses and arrive at your profit or loss. For any tax year, your tax calculation will be based on your profit for the 12 months up to your accounting date which ends in that tax year.

When you start in self-employment it can be worthwhile to fix your accounting year to end on 30 April. This year, for example, that would mean that the profit from the year 1 May 2006 to 30 April 2007 is taxed in the tax year 2007/08. If your accounting year runs from 1 April 2006 to 31 March 2007 (just a month earlier), that income would be taxed a whole year earlier in 2006/07. So by fixing your accounting year to end on 30 April, you in effect put off the tax you pay by almost a year. It also means that you know the exact figures when you come to fill in your tax return.

When a business starts and ends

Special rules apply in the first two years of a new business and when a business ends. For the first year, you are taxed on your profit from the date you start until the following 5 April. For the second year, you are taxed on your profit for the 12 months up to your accounting date in that tax year, provided that the date is at least a year after your business started – if it is not, you are taxed on your profit for the first 12 months of business.

These rules may mean that some part of your profit is taken into account in calculating your taxable profit for more than one tax year. If so, you are entitled to 'overlap relief' when your business ends – the effect being that, over the lifetime of your business, you are taxed on no more and no less than the full amount of your profit. It can get very complicated and it is worth consulting an accountant or tax adviser, at least in the first and last years of your business.

Tax-saving tip: *Choose your accounting date to reduce the tax you pay. When your business starts and ends, get the tax you pay checked carefully by an accountant or tax adviser.*

Business expenses

There is normally no difficulty in deciding how much your business income is, but working out your expenses may be more difficult. The situation is fairly clear-cut if, for example, you are buying goods to resell; but determining other expenses is less straightforward – particularly when expenses are partly for business purposes and partly private.

For example, if you work from home you need a phone. Unless you go to the expense of having a separate business line, your calls will be a mixture of business and personal. The cost of business calls and a share of the phone rental can be deducted from your turnover. To work out the business share, get an itemised bill, which BT and many other phone companies provide at no cost. You can then see the proportion of the costs that are business. There is no need to count them up each time; do it once and then in future you can just charge that proportion of your bill to the business. Keep the evidence in case the Revenue queries it. It is sensible to monitor the position from time to time, especially if the business grows.

You can also charge a proportion of the cost of running your car – including petrol, car tax, and insurance. Keep a note of business and personal mileage to work out the business share.

If you work from home, you will also be able to claim a proportion of domestic expenses. But there are no clear rules about what expenses you can charge or how you work out a fair proportion. You should be able to charge a proportion of gas, electricity, insurance of the contents that are relevant to your business, rent, mortgage interest (but not capital repayments), and Council Tax as a business expense. You may also be able to charge the cost of water if you have a water meter but not otherwise.

The normal way to work out the proportion is to count the main rooms in the house, excluding the bathroom. Some tax inspectors might let you ignore the kitchen too; others may try to count the bathroom. If there are four main rooms and you mainly work from one of them and use that room for little else, then you can charge a quarter of the costs to the business. Alternatively you can measure the floor area of your home and of your office and use that proportion. Whatever method you use, pick one that you think is fair and stick by it.

Tax-saving tip: *Whenever you buy anything for your business (even a newspaper or magazine), or you spend anything on travel (even a bus fare), get a receipt and keep it.*

Capital allowances

The costs of major items, such as a vehicle or office equipment, are normally not all tax-deductible in the year in which you made the expenditure. Instead, tax relief is given through a system of 'capital allowances', which means that the cost of the equipment is spread over a number of years. In 2007/08 you can charge 50% of the cost as an expense in the first year and 25% of the balance in the years after that. The 50% rate does not apply to vehicles such as cars.

The rules and arithmetic of capital allowances are complex, so advice from an accountant or even the Revenue can save you money.

Tax-saving tip: *If you buy anything for your business which will last, you must count it as a capital expense. In 2007/08 you can charge 50% of the cost in year one. The allowance for cars in the first year is normally 25%. But energy-efficient cars in Vehicle Excise Duty band A or B qualify for 100% allowance if you buy them new.*

The system of capital allowances will change in 2008/09. The Government plans to let businesses – including self-employed people – charge 100% of the capital cost of things bought for the business which are 'investing for growth', up to a total of £50,000 in the year. What 'investing for growth' will mean is still not clear. But this new rule will not apply to cars.

Tax-saving tip: *It may be worth putting off a big capital expense, such as a computer or other equipment, until after 6 April 2008 in case that fits into the criterion of investing for growth.*

 The Revenue Self-assessment Help Sheet IR222 gives information about business expenses and capital allowances. You can get a copy from the Revenue Orderline on 08459 000 404 or from the website at www.hmrc.gov.uk/helpsheets/ir222.pdf

Keeping records

On your tax return, you are simply expected to declare total income and expenses. The Revenue does not normally expect to see invoices, receipts, and so on. Nor does it expect to be sent accounts prepared by an accountant. But you must keep proper records of all these things so that you can work out your income and expenditure. You must also keep all your bank or building society statements or passbooks.

It's essential that you have an accounts book, and write it up regularly. If you keep records on your computer, always back up the files and print them out regularly. If you have an internet bank or savings account, print out your statements each month and keep them in a file. Remember to order and keep an annual statement of any interest on savings.

If you are self-employed or rent out property, you are legally obliged to keep all records relating to a particular tax year for five years from the date you filed your return for that year. You can now destroy records for the tax year 2000/01. The tax return for the following year, 2001/02, was due in to the Revenue by 31 January 2003. Five years from then is 31 January 2008. So you can destroy your self-employment records for the tax year 2001/02 on 1 February 2008. But if the Revenue has embarked on an enquiry into your tax affairs, you have to keep the relevant records until that enquiry is finished.

For more details, see the Revenue leaflet SABK4 Self-assessment: A general guide to keeping records, *which is available online at www.hmrc.gov.uk/pdfs/sabk4.pdf*

When tax is paid

Tax on income from self-employment is normally paid in two instalments and a balancing payment. For the 2007/08 tax year, the first instalment will be due on 31 January 2008 and the second on 31 July 2008. If it turns out you have paid too little tax, then a balancing payment will become due on 31 January 2008.

The amount of tax payable under the first two instalments is based upon the amount of tax you were liable to pay for the previous year. Half that amount will normally be due in each instalment. If, however, you believe that your tax will be less than that for the previous year, you can apply to your tax office to have the instalments reduced.

If the total tax due is less than £500, no instalment payments will be required and you can pay all of it on 31 January 2008. If you don't pay the correct amount of tax on the proper date, you will be liable to pay interest on unpaid tax.

Value Added Tax

If you are self-employed or run a small business, you will have to register for VAT if your turnover – which is the total income of your business *not* the profit – exceeds £64,000. Once registered, you must charge VAT at the standard rate (normally 17.5%) on goods or services you supply. Some items are exempt from VAT or zero-rated and you do not have to charge VAT on those and a very few are liable at 5%.

Money-saving tip: *In some circumstances, even if your gross business income does not exceed the £64,000 limit, it may be a good idea to register for VAT. If you register you can recover the VAT on goods or services you buy for business purposes. So get a VAT receipt for everything bought for your business. But registering for VAT will involve you in more paperwork and accounting. So think carefully before doing it.*

The VAT you collect from customers has to be passed on to the Revenue. But you can reclaim the VAT you pay on goods or services you buy. Each quarter (or annually if your turnover is low and you prefer to do it that way) you submit a VAT return showing the amount of VAT collected from your customers and the amount you are reclaiming on goods or services you have bought. You take one from the other and send a cheque for the difference – or make a claim for a refund if you have paid more VAT than you have collected.

Flat-rate scheme

If your taxable turnover excluding VAT is £150,000 or less, you may want to pay your VAT under the flat-rate scheme. Instead of all the fiddly working out of VAT charged and paid, you can pay a flat-rate percentage of your turnover. The percentages range from 4% to 13.5% of your turnover including VAT. The exact rate depends on your business. These rates are reduced by 1% in your first year of trading. The savings can be considerable for some businesses. You can stay in the scheme until your turnover including VAT reaches £225,000 in the year – check that limit on each anniversary of joining the scheme.

Tax-saving tip: *The flat-rate scheme can bring big savings to some businesses. Consider it if your turnover excluding VAT is between £64,000 and £150,000 a year.*

For further information, contact the VAT National Advice Service on 0845 010 9000. A detailed booklet on the flat-rate scheme is Notice 733 from the Revenue or on its website www.hmrc.gov.uk and search on 'Notice 733 Flat Rate Scheme for small businesses'.

Capital Gains Tax

You may have to pay some Capital Gains Tax (CGT) if you sell or give away an asset that has increased in value since you bought it. An 'asset' is something you own, such as shares, antiques, or property. It is not money as such – although in rare circumstances foreign currency may count as an asset. The profit on which you are taxed is called a capital gain.

Major changes in Capital Gains Tax will begin in April 2008. Indexation and tapering (described briefly on pages 87–88) will disappear and the three rates of CGT will be replaced with one rate of 18%. There will be further details of the new rules in the second edition of *Pay Less Tax* that will be published in May 2008.

 Tax-saving tip: *If you are thinking of disposing of anything on which CGT may be due, consider seeking professional advice on whether you should dispose of it before or after 6 April 2008 as the new rules will increase the tax in some cases and cut it in others.*

Not all gains are taxed. Some items are free of CGT:

- your only or main private residence (see pages 88–90);
- private cars;
- National Savings certificates;
- most British Government stocks, usually called 'gilts';
- personal belongings worth up to £6,000;
- individual Savings Accounts (ISAs) and Personal Equity Plans (PEPs);
- proceeds of most life insurance policies;
- Premium Bond prizes, betting winnings, National Lottery winnings; and
- gifts to registered charities.

CGT applies to people who normally live in the UK and consider the UK their home, no matter where in the world their property is located.

There are special rules for business assets which may exempt them from CGT or delay the payment. For more information, look online at www.hmrc.gov.uk/pensioners/ capitalgainstax.htm

How CGT is calculated

Two further exemptions limit the amount that any individual pays in CGT:

- **Any gift you make to a husband, wife, or civil partner with whom you live is entirely free of CGT.** But if they then dispose of the asset, tax is due and will be calculated on the value from the date on which you – not they – acquired it.

- **In the tax year 2007/08 you can have up to**

£9,200 of capital gains without paying tax.
Husbands, wives, and civil partners are taxed
independently on any gains, and each partner is
entitled to a separate exempt amount of £9,200.

Anything above the limit is added to your income
and taxed as though it was sitting on top of your
income – even on top of the top layer of dividends!
Depending on how much other income you have,
your gains will be taxed at either 10%, or 20%, or
40%. Although it is taxed as income, if you have a
low income you cannot use your personal
allowance to reduce a capital gain.

If the asset was bought on 6 April 1998 or later,
then the gain you have made is reduced or
'tapered', depending on how long you have
owned the asset. For example, for non-business
assets owned for five whole years since April
1998, 85% of the gain will be chargeable, and if
they are held for 10 or more whole years the figure
will be 60%.

The Revenue defines 'whole' years as any
continuous 12-month period. It does not have to be
a tax year. If you acquired your asset before 17
March 1988 and still held it at 6 April 1988, you will
get a bonus year's taper relief. There is a more rapid
taper for business assets, but there is no bonus year.

Certain expenses can also be deducted. You can
deduct the costs of acquiring or disposing of the
asset, such as fees to a broker or taxes. You can
also deduct the costs of improving the asset –
such as having a picture professionally restored or
by adding an extension to a let property. Your total
capital gains in a year can be reduced if you have

made capital losses on other things – for example if you sell shares for less than you paid for them.

Losses can be carried forward from one year to the next. If your overall net gain is £9,200 or less, there will be no CGT to pay. But you must set any loss against gains you have made in the same tax year, even if the gains are covered by your annual exemption. A loss made on an asset that is exempt from CGT cannot be claimed.

Tax-saving tip: *If you make a CGT loss, tell the Revenue – otherwise you may not be able to carry it forward.*

If you acquired the asset before April 1998, then a different system called 'indexation' applies to the gain over the period from when you acquired the asset to 5 April 1998. The taper will apply to gains after that date. Assets acquired before 31 March 1982 involve different calculations. If any of that applies to you get help from a qualified tax adviser.

Your home

Capital Gains Tax is not normally charged when you sell or give away the home you live in, as long as:

- it has been your 'main' residence throughout your ownership (even if this condition is not met, you may be entitled to some relief); and
- the grounds do not exceed half a hectare (which is a bit more than one acre).

If you own and live in two properties, you can nominate one of them to be your 'main' residence as long as you have lived in it at some point. You need to do this within two years of acquiring the second property.

If you do have a second property, then the last three years of ownership are exempt from CGT whatever you have used it for, as long as it has been your home at some point. If the other property has been occupied by a dependent relative rent-free since before 6 April 1988, it may be exempt from CGT. A couple who are married or civil partners can have only one 'main residence' between them. Other couples can have one each.

If you separate from your partner or spouse and one of you moves out of the jointly owned home, CGT can arise when the home is sold. It will have to be paid by the partner who moves out, as the home is no longer their main residence. As long as it is sold within three years of the partner moving out, no CGT will be due. After that, some CGT may be due, but the calculation is very complex and you should seek advice.

More information is available from the Low Incomes Tax Reform Group website at www.litrg.org.uk/help/pensioners/ incomesover/life_events_separation.cfm

If you have a lodger – in the home you live in as your main residence – who shares a kitchen and bathroom and living space with you and who lives as a member of the family, you should not have to pay CGT when you sell the property.

But if you let part of your home to someone who does not live as a member of your family, CGT may be payable. That applies even if the rent is exempt from Income Tax under the rent-a-room scheme (see page 4). The gain on which CGT will be calculated is related to the proportion of the property that is rented and the period of letting compared to the total period of ownership. But a certain amount of the gain will normally be exempt, so you may not have to pay any CGT. Ask at your tax office if you need further details.

If you use part of your home exclusively for business purposes, then a proportion of the property may also be liable to CGT when you sell it.

Tax-saving tip: *If you use a room to run a small business or for self-employment, make sure you use it for something else as well, even if only occasionally. That stops the Revenue saying it is used 'exclusively' for business.*

Selling shares

Shares, unit trust units, and shares in OEICs (see pages 31–32) give rise to capital gains or losses when you sell them or give them away. But when you sell or give away shares of the same type, in the same company, that you acquired at different times, there are special rules that govern the way gains and losses are worked out. This doesn't apply to shares or unit trusts held as part of an ISA or a PEP, which are exempt from tax, nor to shares given to charity under the Gift Aid scheme.

If you give shares to someone else who is not your spouse or civil partner, then the difference between the price you paid and their current market value is treated as a capital gain. You may be able to deduct some expenses or apply indexation or taper relief, but if after that the amount exceeds your annual exemption, then you will be liable for CGT.

Windfalls

If you are a member of a building society or a mutual insurance company which changes its status to become a company, then you may well be paid a windfall. That payment is made to compensate you for the value of your membership. The Revenue assumes that you got it for nothing and so the whole amount of the windfall can be counted as a capital gain. If it is big enough, CGT can be due on it. Often, the organisations making these payments will introduce some special device to reduce or avoid this tax. But always check this if you get one.

For more information, see the Revenue leaflet CGT/FS1 Capital Gains Tax: A quick guide *which is available online at www.hmrc.gov.uk/cgt*

Inheritance Tax

Inheritance Tax (IHT) is probably the most hated of the taxes in this book – which is strange because (a) when it is due you are dead; (b) someone else pays it anyway; and (c) the vast majority of people die with too little money and possessions for any IHT to be due.

People fear – and hate – IHT because of the rising price of houses. Many people own a property that is worth enough by itself to mean the tax would be due if they died now. But big changes announced in October 2007 mean that a home owned by a married couple or civil partners is much less likely to exceed the Inheritance Tax threshold. The new rules were announced on 9 October 2007 and began from that date. The law itself, though, will not be changed until the middle of 2008. So the final rules may be different in detail from those announced in 2007. Seek advice before making any changes to your arrangements.

How IHT is calculated

IHT is one of the simpler taxes. In most cases it's quite easy to see if your heirs would have any IHT to pay if you died tomorrow:

£ Add up the value of everything you own, including your house, any investments, savings, personal property, and any payments your heirs will get from life insurance policies which are not written in trust (normally they should be – see pages 100–101 for details on how to do that). Your estate includes all your assets, wherever in the world these are located.

- £ Add to that any substantial gifts you have made in the past seven years, but do not include any gifts covered by the exemptions listed overleaf.

- £ Take away any money owed on a mortgage. If you have raised money on your home, then only count the value of your home minus any debt on it.

- £ Take away any other debts. When you die, unpaid bills, taxes and funeral expenses will be deducted from your estate before it is passed to your heirs.

- £ Take away from the total anything you intend to leave to your spouse or civil partner, or to charity.

- £ If you are in business or farming, there may be further amounts to deduct from the value of the business.

If the final amount is less than the threshold for IHT **no tax will be due**.

In 2007/08 the threshold is £300,000 and will be £312,000 in 2008/09. But when a widowed person dies they may now have a threshold up to twice that amount (see pages 97–99).

If your total is more than this, it is likely that some IHT will be due. It is charged at a single rate of 40% on the excess over the threshold.

- £ So a single person's estate of £400,000 will be taxed at 40% of £100,000 – which is £40,000.

No IHT is due on anything left to your wife or husband or civil partner as long as you both normally live in the UK. Under the new rules which began in October 2007 leaving everything to your spouse is normally the best course.

Ways of reducing IHT

The best way to reduce the IHT that has to be paid is to spend your money now. That way you get to use it and the taxman gets less – and of course so do your heirs. Fortunately (for them) there are other ways of reducing the tax due.

Gifts made more than seven years before your death are completely exempt from IHT. So if you give money away and live another seven years then no IHT will be due on that amount. If you give away more than £300,000 (or whatever the threshold is when you die) before your death, then the tax is reduced on the gifts if you die more than three years after making it.

Other gifts are also not counted even if you do die within seven years of making them, including:

- Gifts to your husband, wife, or civil partner.
- Small gifts of up to £250 each to any number of people.
- Regular gifts out of income that do not reduce your standard of living.
- Wedding gifts of up to £5,000 to your child, or £2,500 to your grandchild or great-grandchild, or £1,000 to anyone else.
- Gifts to a major political party, a registered charity, a national museum or art gallery, or a university.

- Gifts to a child of yours (but not a grandchild) while they are in full-time education if the money is given for their maintenance or the costs of their education or training.
- Other gifts totalling no more than £3,000 in a year. You can also carry this allowance forward from the previous year, so that it can be worth £6,000 if you gave nothing the previous year.

These reliefs and exemptions are personal – so a husband and wife, or two civil partners, can each give these amounts.

> *When **Monica's** husband Stan died she got a considerable pension from his old job. Now he has gone she goes out far less and finds that she never spends her monthly income. Her current account balance rises by about £250 each month. When her granddaughter Jody goes to university, she decides to give her a regular £200 a month. She writes a letter and keeps it with her will saying this is money from her income and does not reduce her standard of living.*

Tax-saving tip: *If they have made no gifts to reduce IHT in the previous year, a couple can give away £12,000 between them in one tax year without it counting for IHT at all. Even if all the assets are owned by one of them, that person can give £6,000 to their spouse or partner, which will be exempt, and then each can give £6,000 to a child.*

Don't give your children or other heirs money that you will need yourself.

Also beware of giving away shares or anything that may have grown in value. If you do, then Capital Gains Tax may be payable on the gain as if you had sold it at market value. It is safer to give away cash.

Some charities try to get you to leave them money in your will as a way of 'tax planning' because the gifts you make are free of Inheritance Tax. Leaving money to charity may be a good thing. But it's not sensible tax planning. Your heirs will in effect be the ones that make the gift.

> **Jane** *dies with an estate of £400,000. She decides to leave £100,000 to charity, so her estate is £300,000 and no IHT is due. Her two children share her £300,000 estate and get £150,000 each.*
>
> *Her neighbour* **Ken** *dies with an identical estate of £400,000. He makes no legacies to charity. His estate is £100,000 above the IHT threshold, so there is £40,000 of tax to pay – leaving a net £360,000 for his two children to share. They get £180,000 each.*

So the heirs do better if you make no legacies to charity. That is simply because 60% of something is better than 100% of nothing. Please leave money to charity. But don't call it tax planning. It isn't.

Your home

For the vast majority of people it is the value of their home which takes their estate into Inheritance Tax territory. Until recently couples were advised to take complicated steps to reduce the tax due so that each left something to their children.

But new rules announced by the Chancellor on 9 October 2007 have changed that advice completely. Now it is normally best to leave everything to your spouse or civil partner.

A widow or widower, or bereaved civil partner, who dies from 9 October 2007 gets their own allowance of £300,000 and their heirs can also add on the unused allowance of the widowed person's late spouse. That means many widows or widowers who die this year will, in effect, have an allowance of £600,000 rather than the £300,000 allowed to single people.

- £ If the first spouse to die leaves nothing to anyone else, then the surviving spouse has an allowance of double the current allowance on her death.

- £ If the first to die has left money or property to other people, then the allowance that can be passed on is reduced.

The calculation is done like this:

- £ The amount they left to people other than their spouse is worked out as a proportion of the allowance that was current at the time. For example, if the first spouse died in 2004/05 when the allowance was £263,000 and they left £50,000 directly to their children, they have used up 50 ÷ 263 or 19% of their allowance. That leaves 81% to be passed on to the survivor.

£ When the surviving spouse dies they get their own allowance plus the unused percentage times the current allowance. So if the second spouse dies this tax year she will get £300,000 as her own allowance and £300,000 x 81% = £243,000 as her inherited allowance, making a total of £543,000. No tax will be due on that amount. Inheritance Tax will be due on anything she leaves above that amount of £543,000.

£ If the first to die leaves property or money to other people which uses up the whole of their allowance then there will be no allowance to pass on to the survivor.

The new rule completely turns on its head advice previously been given to couples. In future, to make the most of the new rules, they should leave everything to their spouse. If they want money, property, or valuables to go to their heirs they should not state that in their will. Instead they should tell their spouse what they would like (and it is safer not to do this in writing) and let the survivor make those gifts later so that they count as lifetime gifts and the rules described earlier will apply. Part of the value may be within one of the tax-free lifetime gifts and if the spouse survives seven years after the gifts are made then no tax will be due. When the second spouse dies, the threshold for IHT will be higher and the estate will get that higher allowance in full twice.

Peter and **Judy** own their family home – which today is worth £575,000 – and Peter had £55,000 in savings but not much else. In May 2005 Peter died. He left the house to Judy but they had agreed he should divide the cash between their two children. As the cash was well below the allowance – then £275,000 – no IHT was due. In August 2008 Judy also dies, leaving the house and her possessions – total £585,000 – to the children.

Peter used up £55,000 or 20% of his £275,000 allowance, leaving 80% for Judy to take over under the new rules. Next year the IHT allowance will be £312,000. When Judy dies her estate willl get that allowance plus another 80% of it, totalling £561,600. Her estate exceeds this by £23,400 so tax is due at 40% on that, which is £9,360.

But if Peter had left everything to Judy and she then gave the maximum exempt amount of £3,000 a year between her children, she would have died with an estate of £631,000. There would have been two allowances due in full, worth £623,000. So the estate exceeds that by only £7,000, leaving tax of £2,800 to pay. That saves £6,560 in tax.

Couples who have already written wills to leave some of their property to children or other heirs should consider rewriting them to leave everything to each other. If they have left property in trust they should seek advice about whether those trust provisions are now necessary or effective. Even after a death a will can usually be rewritten for up to two years if all the heirs agree.

Don't try to avoid tax by giving away something but continuing to benefit from it. For example, if you give away your home but continue to live in it, the value of your home will still count as part of your estate even if the legal title actually belongs to someone else – such as one of your children.

If you live with someone to whom you are not married (and you are not civil partners), there is no IHT exemption on gifts or inheritance between you. So if your home is worth more than the IHT threshold of £300,000 (2007/08) and the one who owns the house dies, the surviving partner can face a big IHT bill just to remain in the home. (The Revenue will let you pay the tax due on a property in ten annual instalments but interest will be charged.) That can also happen if you own half each and the property is worth more than twice the IHT threshold. There is little you can do about this danger, but you should be aware of it.

In Scotland a new status of 'cohabitant' has been created but, although this gives unmarried couples some rights to each other's property on separation or death, it does not help with Inheritance Tax.

Other ways to avoid the tax

If you have a life insurance policy that pays out on your death, make sure that the policy is 'written in trust'. This means that the proceeds do not go directly to your dependants. Instead they are paid into a trust, which then passes them on to your dependants – that avoids the proceeds counting as part of your estate. But if the value of the policy is more than £300,000, then some tax may be due from time to time.

If your policy is worth more than £300,000, consult your insurer or an accountant.

Trusts can be a way to avoid IHT but they can be expensive to set up and run, and are mainly suitable for people with estates worth considerably more than the IHT limit of £300,000. New restrictions mean they are less useful than they were in the past and the Government may restrict their use again.

Some insurance companies and financial consultants sell plans to reduce or avoid Inheritance Tax. Such schemes can be complicated – juggling the ownership of money or making gifts into or from trusts – and frequently involve taking out an insurance policy. These schemes are often designed to generate commission for the salesperson rather than benefit you. The Government has taken action to stop some of these schemes working, and it has warned that it will take action against any scheme that achieves nothing but the reduction of tax. Before committing yourself to any scheme, be sure it has the approval of the Revenue, and discuss it with an impartial professional adviser such as a solicitor or accountant. They are best avoided.

For more information, see the Revenue website (at www.hmrc.gov.uk/cto/ customerguide/page1.htm). You can contact the Probate and IHT Helpline on 0845 30 20 900.

Stamp Duty Land Tax

One of the latest wheezes to part us from our money is Stamp Duty Land Tax. When it was just known as 'stamp duty' it was paid by a very few people buying very expensive property. Now it is paid by most people when they buy a home and it brings in billions a year for the Government.

When you buy a house or flat for more than £125,000, Stamp Duty Land Tax (SDLT) will normally be due. The rates of SDLT are:

Price of property	Rate of tax
Up to £125,000	Nil
£125,001 to £250,000	1% of total price
£250,001 to £500,000	3% of total price
£500,001 and above	4% of total price

The tax is calculated on the total price.

- £ So the tax on a home sold for £250,000 is 1%, which equals £2,500.
- £ But the SDLT due on a home sold for £250,001 is 3%, which equals £7,505 – an extra £5,005 tax for an extra £1 on the price!

Just to make it that bit more expensive, SDLT is always rounded up to the next £5.

Tax-saving tip: *If you are buying a home on which SDLT will be due, you can reduce the tax by negotiating with the owner to buy things such as carpets, curtains, and other movable fittings separately – no tax will be due on those amounts. But don't try to pay more than they are worth. This tip can be particularly useful if you are buying the property for just above one of the thresholds and you can bring the price down below that.*

In some parts of the country – designated as 'disadvantaged', though some of them are very good to live in – the nil rate of SDLT applies up to £150,000, not £125,000.

To see whether the property you are buying is in a 'disadvantaged' area, you can check on the Revenue website (www.hmrc.gov.uk/so), where there is a lot of other information about SDLT.

Tax-saving tip: *If you are buying a property for between £125,000 and £150,000, check its postcode to see if it is in a 'disadvantaged' area. You could save up to £1,500.*

Tax allowances and rates
2006/07 & 2007/08

Allowances

Personal allowances		
Age	**2006/07**	**2007/08**
Under 65	£5,035	£5,225
65 to 74*	£7,280	£7,550
75 or more*	£7,420	£7,690
Blind person	£1,660	£1,730

*Age at 5 April 2008

Age-related allowances are reduced if total income is more than £20,900 in 2007/08 or £20,100 in 2006/07. The reduction is £1 for each £2 above the limits. The over 65 allowances are not reduced below the under 65 allowance.

Married Couple's Allowance		
Age	**2006/07**	
	Amount	Deduction
72** to 74*	£6,065	£606.50
75 or more*	£6,135	£613.50
Minimum amount	£2,350	£235.00

*Age at 5 April 2008
**Older partner must have been born before 6 April 1935

Married Couple's Allowance		
Age	**2007/08**	
	Amount	Deduction
72** to 74*	£6,285	£628.50
75 or more*	£6,365	£636.50
Minimum amount	£2,440	£244.00

*Age at 5 April 2008
**Older partner must have been born before 6 April 1935

The Married Couple's Allowance is not a true tax allowance. An amount equal to 10% of it is deducted from the tax due. Those amounts are shown in the tables above.

If income is high enough to reduce the age allowance to the under 65 rate, the Married Couple's Allowance is reduced at the same rate but it is never reduced below the minimum amount.

Tax rates and bands

Tax bands – income above personal allowances

	2006/07
Starting rate applies to	First £2,150
Basic rate applies to	Next £2,151 to £33,300
Higher-rate applies to	Income above £33,300

Tax bands – income above personal allowances

	2007/08
Starting rate applies to	First £2,230
Basic rate applies to	Next £2,231 to £34,600
Higher-rate applies to	Income above £34,600

Tax rates on income bands

	2006/07	2007/08
Starting rate – all income	10%	10%
Basic rate – dividends	10%	10%
Basic rate – interest	20%	20%
Basic rate – other income	22%	22%
Higher-rate – dividends	32.5%	32.5%
Higher-rate – all other income	40%	40%

Dividends are treated as the top slice of income; interest and other investment income next; and all other income as the bottom slice when tax is being calculated.

These allowances, bands and rates will change considerably in 2008/09.

More help

Her Majesty's Revenue & Customs (HMRC: the Revenue)
Look under 'HM Revenue & Customs in the business listings section of your local phone book. If it is not there, try under 'Inland Revenue …' which is where it used to be.
Taxback: 0845 077 6543
Pay less tax on your savings: 0845 980 0645
www.hmrc.gov.uk
Everything you need to know about tax in the UK, though not always as clear or easy to find your way around as it might be.

CAPITAL TAXES

England and Wales
Ferrers House
PO Box 38
Castle Meadow Rd
Nottingham
NG2 1BB

Scotland
Meldrum House
15 Drumsheugh
Gardens
Edinburgh
EH3 7QG

Northern Ireland
Level 3
Dorchester House
52–58 Great Victoria St
Belfast BT2 7QL

Probate and IHT Helpline: 0845 30 20 900
Orderline: 0845 234 1000
For current information about Capital Gains Tax and Inheritance Tax.

Chartered Institute of Taxation
12 Upper Belgrave Street
London SW1X 8BB
020 7235 9381
www.tax.org.uk
Professional body for tax advisers.

Directgov
www.direct.gov.uk
This website is the one-stop shop for all information on government services in the UK, including details on benefits, social security and tax.

Disability and Carers Service
0800 88 22 00
www.dwp.gov.uk/lifeeve
nt/benefits/dcs
The part of the Department for Work and Pensions that deals with benefits and services for disabled people and their carers. There are ten centres around the country.

Entitled To
www.entitledto.com
A website that works out entitlement to means-tested benefits, including Pension Credit, tax credits, Council Tax Benefit and Housing Benefit.

Institute of Chartered Accountants in England and Wales
Chartered Accountants' Hall
PO Box 433
London EC2P 2BJ
020 7920 8100
www.icaew.co.uk
For information about choosing and using a chartered accountant. For Scotland, ring 0131 347 0100 or see the website at www.icas.org.uk

Land Registry
32 Lincoln's Inn Fields
London WC2A 3PH
020 7917 8888
www.landreg.gov.uk
For information in England and Wales about how to change ownership if you are joint tenants.

Low Incomes Tax Reform Group

12 Upper Belgrave Street
London SW1X 8BB
020 7235 9381
Helpline: 0845 601 3321
www.litrg.org.uk
Aims to give a voice to those on low incomes who have been unfairly treated by the tax or tax-credit authorities, and lobbies for simplification of the tax system. Probably the best tax and tax credits website for those on low incomes.

The Pension Service

0845 60 60 265
www.thepensionservice.
gov.uk
The part of the Department for Work and Pensions that deals with pensions.

Registers of Scotland

Erskine House
68 Queen Street
Edinburgh EH2 4NF
0845 607 0161
www.ros.gov.uk
For information about how to change

ownership if you are joint owners with survivorship in Scotland.

TaxAid

0845 120 3779
(10am–noon,
Mondays–Thursdays)
www.taxaid.org.uk
Offers free advice, on the phone or by appointment only, to people with tax problems who cannot afford an accountant.

TaxHelp for Older People

Pineapple Business Park
Salway Ash
Bridport
Dorset DT6 5DB
0845 601 3321
www.taxvol.org.uk
Independent free tax advice service by tax professionals for older people on low incomes.

Index

About Age Concern

Age Concern is the UK's largest organisation working for and with older people to enable them to make more of life. We are a federation of over 400 independent charities who share the same name, values and standards and believe that later life should be fulfilling, enjoyable and productive.

Age Concern England
1268 London Road
London SW16 4ER
SW16 4ER
Tel: 020 8765 7200
www.ageconcern.org.uk

Age Concern Cymru
Ty John Pathy
Units 13 and 14 Neptune Court
Vanguard Way, Cardiff CF24 5PJ
Tel: 029 2043 1555
www.accymru.org.uk

Age Concern Scotland
Causewayside House
160 Causewayside
Edinburgh EH9 1PP
Tel: 0845 833 0200
www.ageconcernscotland.org.uk

Age Concern Northern Ireland
3 Lower Crescent
Belfast BT7 1NR
Tel: 028 9024 5729
www.ageconcernni.org

Age Concern Books

Age Concern publishes a wide range of bestselling books that help thousands of people each year. They provide practical, trusted advice on subjects ranging from pensions and planning for retirement, to using a computer and surfing the internet. Whether you are caring for someone with a health problem or want to know more about your rights to healthcare, we have something for everyone.

Ordering is easy To order any of our books or request our free catalogue simply choose one of the following options:

☎ Call us on **0870 44 22 120**

🖱 Visit our website at **www.ageconcern.org.uk/bookshop**

📧 Email us at **sales@ageconcernbooks.co.uk**

You can also buy our books from all good bookshops.

Another great book from Age Concern...

Your Rights to Money Benefits 07/08
Age Concern's bestselling guide
Sally West

'If you buy one book about finances, make it this one'
Choice Magazine, 2007

'Essential' *Daily Express*

Nearly £4 billion in benefits goes unclaimed every year, which means that millions of older people are missing out on money that is rightfully theirs. If you think you – or someone you know – could be one of them, Age Concern's bestselling guide is for you. With over 3 million copies sold, this annually updated book has the most accurate information on the range of benefits available for people in retirement. At only £5.99, this could be the wisest investment you make this year.

£5.99 • Paperback • 978-0-86242-427-5

Ordering is easy

To order any of our books or request our free catalogue simply choose one of the following options:

☎ **Call us on 0870 44 22 120**

🖱 **Visit our website at
www.ageconcern.org.uk/bookshop**

✉ **Email us at sales@ageconcernbooks.co.uk**

You can also buy our books from all good bookshops.